Legal Issues & Education Technology: A School Leader's Guide

Second Edition

Edwin C. Darden

Editor

A Technology Leadership Network Special Report

ITTE: Education Technology Programs
National School Boards Association
Alexandria, Virginia

Copyright © 2001 National School Boards Association
All rights reserved
Printed in the United States
International Standard Book Number: 0-88364-247-6

National School Boards Association
1680 Duke Street
Alexandria, Virginia 22314-3493
phone: 703-838-6722
fax: 703-683-7590
E-mail: info@nsba.org
URL: www.nsba.org

Legal Issues & Educational Technology: A School Leader's Guide, Second Edition
may be ordered from the NSBA Distribution Center, 1-800-706-6722,
order # 03-150-44. Single copy: $28 members (Technology Leadership Network,
National Affiliates); $35 (non-members). Bulk discounts available.

Cite as:

Darden, Edwin C. ed. 2001. *Legal issues & education technology: A school leader's guide.*
2nd ed. Alexandria, VA: National School Boards Association.

Editor: Ismat Abdal-Haqq, NSBA

Design: William Maxwell, WM Graphics, Washington, DC

Production Manager: Gerry Freiert, NSBA

·NSBA·

Dear Education Leader:

The National School Boards Association is pleased to present the second edition of this valuable resource, *Legal Issues & Education Technology: A School Leader's Guide,* written by members of the NSBA Council of School Attorneys (COSA) and produced by NSBA's ITTE: Education Technology Programs (ITTE).

This publication focuses on preventive strategies school leaders need to avoid costly and disruptive litigation that may result from incautious implementation or administration of technology in schools. The contents reflect recent legislation and court decisions and are presented in an easy to read format. Topics include: Internet filters; legal requirements for accessible Web design and ergonomically sound facilities; student and staff privacy rights; COPPA, CIPA, FERPA, and ADA compliance issues and updates; copyright; acceptable use policies; off-site data storage policies; commercial agreements with e-businesses; open-meeting "sunshine" laws; and more.

Legal Issues & Education Technology: A School Leader's Guide, Second Edition is the latest in a series of special reports published by ITTE, which sponsors publications, meetings, site visits, electronic communities, Web sites, and conferences to promote constructive and responsible use of education technology. More than 500 school districts in the United States and Canada participate in ITTE's Technology Leadership Network.

COSA provides leadership in legal advocacy for public schools and information and practical assistance to more than 3,000 attorneys representing school boards. COSA focuses on prevention of lawsuits in public schools, supports NSBA's legal advocacy efforts, and provides continuing legal education and specialized publications.

We invite you to call on NSBA, ITTE, and COSA for additional resources to assist you in planning and implementing programs that use technology to promote student learning and support the work of school boards, administrators, and practitioners.

Sincerely,

James R. Ruhland
President, NSBA

Anne L. Bryant
Executive Director, NSBA

Cynthia Lutz Kelly
Chairman, COSA

National School Boards Association
2001-2002 Board of Directors

President
James R. Ruhland*

President-Elect
Mossi W. White*

Secretary-Treasurer
Carol C. Brown*

Immediate Past President
Clarice L. Chambers*

DIRECTORS

Pamela Betheil*
Barbara L. Bolas
Margie T. Bradford
George E. Evans
E. Jane Gallucci
Juanita Haugen
Sandra J. Jensen
Robert A. Lane
George H. McShan*
William R. Meek
Becky Montgomery
Joan E. Schmidt
James R. Vanderlin
Janet Watson
Norman Wooten

Ex Officio **Voting Directors**

Florence D. Johnson
Chair, Council of Urban Boards
of Education

Robert L. Ochoa
President, National Caucus of
Hispanic School Board Members

Ernest H. White, Jr.*
President, National Caucus of
Black School Board Members

Ex Officio **Non-Voting Directors**

Anne L. Bryant*
NSBA Executive Director

Cynthia Lutz Kelly
Chair, Council of School Attorneys

Sandra Sims de-Graffenried**
Chair, Federation Member Executive
Directors' Liaison Committee

* Executive Committee Member
** Executive Committee Observer

about NSBA...

The National School Boards Association is the nationwide organization representing public school governance. NSBA's mission is to foster excellence and equity in public elementary and secondary education through school board leadership. NSBA achieves its mission by representing the school board perspective before federal government agencies and with national organizations that affect education, and by providing vital information and services to state associations of school boards and local school boards throughout the nation.

NSBA advocates local school boards as the ultimate expression of grassroots democracy. NSBA supports the capacity of each school board—acting on behalf of and in close concert with the people of its community—to envision the future of education in its community, to establish a structure and environment that allow all students to reach their maximum potential, to provide accountability for the people of its community on performance in the schools, and to serve as the key community advocate for children and youth and their public schools.

Founded in 1940, NSBA is a not-for-profit federation of associations of school boards across the United States and its territories. NSBA represents the nation's 95,000 school board members that govern 14,890 local school districts serving the nation's more than 47 million public school students. Virtually all school board members are elected; the rest are appointed by elected officials.

NSBA policy is determined by a 150-member Delegate Assembly of local school board members. The 25-member Board of Directors translates this policy into action. Programs and services are administered by the NSBA executive director and a 150-person staff. NSBA is located in metropolitan Washington, D.C.

NSBA's Programs and Services

- **National Affiliate Program** – enables school boards to work with their state association and NSBA to identify and influence federal and national trends and issues affecting public school governance.
- **Council of Urban Boards of Education** – serves the governance needs of urban school boards.
- **Large District Forum** – serves the governance needs of large but non-urban boards.
- **Rural and Small District Forum** – serves the governance needs of rural and small enrollment districts.
- **Federal Relations Network** – school board members from each congressional district actively participate in NSBA's federal and national advocacy efforts.
- **Federal Policy Coordinators Network** – focuses on the administration of federally funded programs.
- **Award Winning Publications** – *American School Board Journal, School Board News,* and special substantive reports on public school governance throughout the year.
- **ITTE: Education Technology Programs and Technology Leadership Network** – advance public education through best uses of technology in the classroom and school district operations.
- **Council of School Attorneys** – focuses on school law issues and services to school board attorneys.
- **Annual Conference and Exposition** – the nation's largest policy and training conference for local education officials on national and federal issues affecting the public schools in the United States.
- **National Education Policy Network** – provides the latest policy information nationwide and a framework for public governance through written policies.
- **Training/Development and Resource Exchange** – meetings, online clearinghouse and consulting services to develop leadership of state school boards associations and local school boards.

National School Boards Association
1680 Duke Street, Alexandria, VA 22314-3493
Phone: 703-838-6722   Fax: 703-683-7590
Web Address: http://www.nsba.org   E-mail: info@nsba.org

Excellence and Equity in Public Education through School Board Leadership   2/9/01

About the NSBA ITTE:
Education Technology Programs

The National School Boards Association established the ITTE: Education Technology Programs (formerly known as the Institute for the Transfer of Technology to Education) in 1985 to advance the wise and appropriate use of technology in public education. The Technology Leadership Network, a major component of ITTE, was created in 1986 to help school districts share in dialogue about technology in education.

Special reports such as this one are among the benefits of participation in the Technology Leadership Network. The newsletter *Technology Leadership News*, the annual Technology + Learning Conference, site visits to exemplary school districts, topical meetings, and an e-mail list are some of the additional opportunities.

For information on events, activities, publications, and more than 450 school districts participating in the Technology Leadership Network, see ITTE's Web site, www.nsba.org/itte, or contact the ITTE staff at NSBA, 1680 Duke St., Alexandria, VA 22314, (703) 838-6722, e-mail:itte@nsba.org.

About the NSBA Council of School Attorneys

Leadership in legal advocacy for public schools has been the overriding mission of the NSBA Council of School Attorneys throughout its celebrated history. Almost 3,000 members strong today, the Council was formed in 1967 to provide information and practical assistance to attorneys who represent public school districts. It is the only national advocacy organization composed exclusively of attorneys representing school boards. It offers continuing legal education, specialized publications, a forum for exchange of information, and it supports the legal advocacy efforts of the National School Boards Association. For information on membership, contact your state school boards association or the NSBA Council of School Attorneys.

The Council accepts individual attorney members from unaffiliated states and has an affiliate member agreement with the following state attorneys' councils: Alabama, Arizona, Arkansas, California, Colorado, Delaware, Florida, Georgia, Illinois, Iowa, Kansas, Louisiana, Maine, Maryland, Massachusetts, Michigan, Mississippi, Missouri, Montana, Nebraska, New Hampshire, New Jersey, New Mexico, New York, North Carolina, North Dakota, Oklahoma, Oregon, Pennsylvania, South Carolina, South Dakota, Tennessee, Texas, Virginia, and West Virginia. URL: http://www.nsba.org/cosa

Contents

Introduction

In December 2000, the U.S. Department of Education released its second national education technology plan, *e-Learning: Putting a World Class Education at the Fingertips of All Children*. A statement from then Secretary of Education Richard Riley introduced the five National Educational Technology Goals, which are at the core of the plan: "This debate has never been about technology. It has been about what our children have the opportunity to do. It's about connecting students to a whole new world of learning resources and offering the mind the opportunity to expand and take on a new and challenging future."

> *"This debate has never been about technology. It has been about what our children have the opportunity to do. It's about connecting students to a whole new world of learning resources and offering the mind the opportunity to expand and take on a new and challenging future."*
>
> *Richard W. Riley,*
> *Former Secretary of Education*
> *e-Learning: Putting a World Class Education at the Fingertips of All Children, 2000 "*

It has becoming increasingly apparent that bringing into schools the technologies that provide opportunities for students and teachers to expand their minds and connect to the "new world of learning resources" can produce profound changes in the school environment—changes in relationships, capacity, authority, roles, instructional practice, and the very nature of schooling. It has also become apparent that the advent of the new technologies sometimes challenges the laws, policies, regulations, and practices that govern and support that environment.

School leaders find themselves wrestling with evolving definitions of intellectual property, student privacy, security, and other issues being shaped by technological change. As stewards of the children in their schools and the district resources under their supervision, they struggle to protect students and staff and shield their districts from liability without diminishing the enabling power of the technological assets within those schools.

Legal Issues & Education Technology: A School Leader's Guide, 2nd Edition helps school leaders achieve a workable balance that allows schools to take advantage of the educational and administrative benefits of digital technologies while protecting the district from disruptive and expensive litigation.

Chapter 1, "Student Learning and the Law of School Technology," focuses on developing policies and practices for regulating student use of e-mail, the Internet, and the World Wide Web. It outlines relevant statutes, provides up-to-date information from recent legislation and case law, and covers acceptable use policies, protecting students from inappropriate online material, student privacy, school-business relationships, and virtual schools.

Chapter 2, "Administrative Issues in School Technology," addresses school district liabilities in areas such as sexual harassment and universal access for persons with

disabilities. It deals with the use of e-mail as evidence in litigation, attorney-client privilege in electronic communication, and how school board members can avoid violating open meetings laws while engaging in electronic exchanges.

Chapter 3, "Legal Considerations in Regulating Employee Use of School Technology," addresses several issues related to staff access to computers—personal use and privacy, collective bargaining, First Amendment concerns, and employee safety.

Chapter 4, "Copyright Law," reviews fundamental principles of copyright law that educators are likely to encounter when dealing with digital technologies. It also provides guidelines for copyright policies and procedures.

Each chapter concludes with a resource list. Throughout *Legal Issues & Education Technology: A School Leader's Guide, 2nd Edition*, there are templates and sample language and policies. More are found in the appendices. Also found after the chapters is a glossary of terms used in the book.

NSBA has revised and updated the first edition of *Legal Issues & Education Technology: A School Leader's Guide*, published in 1999 and no longer in print. The new edition reflects recent court decisions and the latest federal regulations and statutes. It also incorporates illustrations from schools and districts.

This guide can help school board members, superintendents and district administrators, technology coordinators, principals, and teachers understand how to comply with laws that relate to technology use in schools. Its thrust is preventive. It alerts school leaders to the challenges that emerge when schools and digital technology intersect, and it assists school leaders in crafting policies and procedures to shield their districts from liability.

Chapter 1

Student Learning & the Law of School Technology

Ronald D. Wenkart, Esq.
General Counsel, Orange County, California Department of Education
and Edwin C. Darden, Esq.
Senior Staff Attorney, National School Boards Association

Introduction

Public school access to the Internet, e-mail, and other digital technologies offers students exciting opportunities for self-directed learning and access to countless resources. These technologies supply tools that increase productivity, stimulate creativity, and help bridge geographic and cultural divides. However, their presence in public schools also introduces a number of complex legal issues.

Competing interests are often a factor. For example, student e-mail exchanges and student-produced Web pages may create dilemmas where the student's right to privacy and free speech must be weighed against the interests of parents and the school district.

This chapter helps school leaders develop and implement student technology use policies that support student learning, protect the school community, and comply with existing laws. It begins with a discussion of acceptable use policies—why they are important and what they should include. Without endorsing any one approach, it discusses elements that will produce a policy that can enhance student achievement and be the saving grace if litigation occurs. Next, the extent to which schools can discipline students for actions related to off-campus student Web sites will be considered. Other topics include: posting student information on school-sponsored Web sites; monitoring student e-mail; filtering and blocking access to inappropriate online material and the Children's Internet Protection Act (CIPA); protecting student privacy under the Family Educational Rights and Privacy Act (FERPA); and equal access issues, including complying with the Americans with Disabilities Act (ADA). Finally, the chapter examines the use of surveillance technologies to detect plagiarism, misconduct, and crimes; e-commerce and online advertising; and virtual schools.

Acceptable Use Policy

An acceptable use policy (AUP) is the natural starting point for developing a comprehensive and coherent approach to student Internet and technology access. Such a policy—distributed widely to parents, teachers, staff, the community, and, via the Internet, to the world—can act as both a billboard and a shield. A well-designed AUP clearly explains the school district's expectation that technology should be used to further student achievement and sets forth conditions under which students are allowed to use the Internet and school technology.

Currently, most school districts essentially have no choice about having an acceptable use policy in place. The Children's Internet Protection Act (CIPA), signed into law in December 2000, was passed by Congress to protect children from inappropriate online material. Among its provisions, CIPA requires school districts receiving E-rate funds to install filtering and blocking software and have a board of education-approved AUP. Furthermore, some states, such as California, Virginia, and Indiana, make acceptable use policies mandatory by law.

A sound policy:

- puts parents and students on notice about the rules for acceptable use of school technology

- diminishes parents' and students' expectation that electronic communications are private

- establishes parameters for acceptable student behavior while using school technology

- allows school officials to discipline those who violate the terms of the policy

- specifies that school personnel will, to the extent possible, supervise technology access

This approach in important becomes the contract between the school, the student, and the parent or guardian. Districts must be unequivocally clear that access to the "international network of inter-connected computers"—commonly known as the Internet—is a privilege and not a right. Permission to use school technology, therefore, will be withdrawn if there is a violation of rules, policies, or generally accepted conventions. Legally, it puts everyone on notice as to "acceptable use," and it helps protect the school against later claims. Districts that provide school equipment or resources to students and teachers off campus should make it a top priority to notify students, parents, and teachers that the acceptable use policy applies beyond the confines of the school campus and that abuse or misuse will be punished as if it occurred on campus if school equipment is involved.

An AUP is the most important ingredient in a school district's formula for regulating technology use. In crafting the policy, the key, it seems, is striking a healthy balance between the need to protect the school district from potential liability—risk management—and harnessing the power of digital technologies to advance teaching and learning.

Striking the balance is not necessarily a 50-50 proposition. Unless there is reason to believe otherwise, the working assumption of school officials should be that most students will responsibly handle e-mail, the Internet, personal computers/personal digital assistants on loan, other hardware, and software. As in other policy areas, an infraction is thus an exception that can be dealt with on a case-by-case basis. The core part of the rule then, is built to maximize the educational value, perhaps sacrificing somewhat the urge to minimize legal exposure.

While it is best to address specific topics, such as the right of school personnel to review browser logs (which track the Web sites students have viewed), school officials and attorneys may want to consider leaving the language flexible enough to cover unforeseen circumstances and issues that arise in the course of student use. One common mistake is trying to be as broad as possible, resulting in language that is vague and may not survive federal court scrutiny.

Students within a school setting still have constitutional free speech rights, and an acceptable use policy that constricts those rights unnecessarily may be subject to a First Amendment challenge. A statement like "students shall not have access to unacceptable or offensive material" may sound good in the abstract, but a court may view it as vague and without real meaning. If so, the court might declare it unconstitutional because readers and users were not placed on fair notice of what was permissible and what was not. Furthermore, the court may say such language is overbroad, sweeping into its scope a number of topics that ought to be protected by free speech principles.

Because of the fast-changing nature of technology, it is advisable to review the acceptable use policy each year. Even if no revisions are made, the review creates an opportunity for the school board, technology experts, and the school or district attorney to assure that nothing within the policy has been outstripped by technological advance or the increasing number of court cases in this area.

Finally, school districts face the question of whether to have a single policy, which covers both students and school district employees, or to create separate policies. The choice is largely a matter of philosophical and practical preferences and a decision that officials should discuss with their attorneys. Each approach has its advantages and disadvantages. For example, a single policy allows for a single standard for everyone and avoids confusion about which rules apply to which populations. Separate policies, however, allow a district to tailor the policies to the specific needs and circumstances unique to students on the one hand and workers on the other. [A separate employee policy is advocated in Chapter 3: *Legal Considerations in Regulating Employee Use of School Technology*.]

Discipline Policies Governing Off-Campus Student Web Sites

A key consideration for the prudent school district is whether the acceptable use policy or the general discipline policy will specifically seek to punish students for off-campus behavior that either causes or has the potential for causing on-campus disturbances. For example, what action can a school district take against a student who creates a "hate site" featuring a loathed teacher, a nemesis classmate, or the guy who refused to ask her out for a date? What if the student site includes sexually explicit matter and is linked back to the official school site?

Over the last two years there has been an explosion in the number of such incidents. Upset, school administrators sometimes act in haste without evaluating the legal issues or whether disciplinary action is appropriate. To avoid the problems that may ensue as a consequence of unconsidered reactions, school districts should anticipate similar occurrences and determine a proper response.

If the student is not using the district computer or server, linking to the school district, calling up the offensive site at school, or otherwise drawing a school connection, the district may find itself in the midst of a classic clash between the student's First Amendment right of free speech under the United States Constitution and the equally important responsibility of the school district to maintain a safe and proper learning environment. What is most vexing about this topic is that there is still no seminal case, no definitive guidance that school attorneys or school officials can look to for parameters. In its absence, we must look to the few state and federal court cases on record and try to anticipate other courts' actions, based on sound principles. The U.S. Supreme Court has not dealt with the issue of student Internet speech off campus; and as of mid-2001, no clear prospect for such a decision was on the horizon.

On the student side, there are the free speech principles that protect any U.S. citizen who seeks to express an opinion – regardless of how heinous or immature. The Internet in particular is seen as the free marketplace of ideas and has been dubbed so by the U.S. Supreme Court.[1]

Elements of an Effective "Acceptable Use" Policy Governing Student Internet Access

1. Establishes clear parameters and detailed ground rules on when and how students can use the Internet—whether at school or at home.

2. Contains an annual notification clause that requires parents or guardians at the start of each school year to grant explicit permission for their child to use the school-provided Internet service. The implementing document should also require the child's signature with both parties acknowledging that the policy has been read and understood and will be complied with.

3. Asserts the rights of the school district to censor the content of material that students read based on legitimate pedagogical concerns.

4. Explains to parents that, as with other matters, teachers and administrators have a duty to supervise at all times the conduct of the children on the school grounds and to enforce those rules and regulations necessary to their protection. The policy should also contain a disclaimer of sorts and enlist parent support for enforcement.

   E.g. "Although student use of the Internet while at school will be supervised by staff, we cannot guarantee that students will not gain access to inappropriate materials. We encourage parents to have a discussion with their children about values and how those beliefs should guide student activities while using the Internet." — Eugene, Oregon School Policy

5. Makes compliance part of the student code of conduct and subject to discipline for willful violations.

6. Prohibits obscenity or other offensive language while using school equipment.

7. Makes reference to applicable copyright laws and pledges compliance with them as part of student use.

8. Prohibits the use of the Internet by students for financial gain.

9. Forewarns students that network storage areas may be treated like school lockers. Network administrators may review files and communications to maintain system integrity and insure that users are using the system responsibly. Users should not expect that files stored on district servers will always be private.

The school district has on its side the *Tinker v. Des Moines Community School District* [2] case, which stands for the principle that while students have free speech rights on school grounds, they do not have the right to engage in conduct that causes a material and substantial disruption in school operations or has the reasonable potential to do so. The argument that an off-campus Web site creation warrants discipline has to meet both the disruption standard and draw a clear nexus (or direct connection) between the conduct and what happens at school.

Schools should also consider the lessons learned in *Bethel School District No. 403 v. Fraser* [3] about the ability of school districts to limit profanity and sexual innuendo in school speeches for student office and *Hazelwood v. Kuhlmeier* [4] about the power of school officials to limit student newspaper subjects for pedagogical reasons.

One effective way of approaching the issue is to assign the questionable Web site content to one of three categories of speech:

- Category 1 – Are the contents of the Web site simply offensive, obnoxious, and insulting?

- Category 2 – Do the contents mirror Category 1 but add a veiled threat or incite others to violence or lawlessness?

- Category 3 – Is there an outright threat to person or property?

If the speech falls within Category 1, while it may be hurtful to an employee or student, it is likely beyond the reach of school discipline and will be shielded by the First Amendment. That is not to say, however, that individuals cannot file private lawsuits to soothe their indignation.

Category 2 content creates a closer call, and school officials and their attorneys will have to make judgment on a case-by-case basis. Part of the analysis will be the student involved, the credibility of the veiled threat itself, and the likelihood that others might be goaded into violence.

To the authors, Category 3 Web site content, with explicit threats, conveys no ambiguity at all. Given the level of school violence that has been carried out in recent years, any outright threat of violence, typically, has earned a swift and sure response under the school district's discipline code.

But placing the Web site into the right category is only half the battle. The other half—drawing a connection between the conduct and the school district—is also a necessary element to overcome a constitutional free speech challenge by the site's student creator.

To do so, a school district might evaluate the following factors:

- Does the Web site link to the school district's official Web site?

- Has the student creator or another student accessed the Web page on district equipment or even while on campus?

- Have students or faculty changed their behavior in any way in response to the Web site's content?

- Does the school district have a Web design course that the student might have taken, meaning they learned the skills to construct the Web site while at school?

- Has the student interfered with the academic program in any way—for example, by disclosing answers to exams?

Off-Campus Student Web Sites: Recent Court Cases

Perhaps the most well-known recent case, and probably the most legally significant, came from Missouri in late 1998. A federal district court found in favor of Brandon Beussink, a student, granting him a preliminary injunction to block the district's 10-day suspension. Beussink had created a Web site at home that said critical things about the school district and some of the people at school. He then linked his page to the official district home page. Fearing disruption, school officials called on him to halt the practice. The case was settled on terms favorable to Beussink shortly before the trial began in the summer of 1999.[5]

In a case decided in 1999, high school student Karl Beidler was suspended for posting negative information about the assistant principal. A Thurston County (Washington) Superior Court Judge ruled that public school officials could not punish the student for speech that occurred away from school. Under a court-approved agreement, the school district was ordered to pay $10,000 in damages and more than $50,000 in attorneys' fees in connection with the incident.

J.S., an eighth-grade student, created on his home computer a Web site called "Teacher Sux," which consisted of derogatory comments about his algebra teacher and the school principal in the Bethlehem Area School District in Pennsylvania. The site featured a picture of his math teacher that morphed into Hitler, sought donations of $20 to help J.S. pay for a hit man, and showed a diagram of the teacher with her head cut off and blood dripping from her neck. The Commonwealth Court of Pennsylvania thought that went too far. In a 2000 opinion, the court stated, "Regrettably, in this day and age when school violence is becoming more commonplace, school officials are justified in taking very seriously threats against faculty and other students. Given the contents of Student's web-site and the effect it had upon Mr. Kartsotis, Mrs. Fulmer and the school community, we conclude that the trial court properly determined that the School District did not violate Student's rights under the First Amendment."[6]

Nick Emmett, a student at Kentlake High School in the state of Washington created the "Unofficial Kentlake High Home Page" where he created mock "obituaries" about several of his friends. He then asked visitors to the site to vote on who would be the next classmate to "die" and be featured in an obituary. A local television station broadcast a report that Emmett had created a "hit list" of people he was planning to kill. The boy was disciplined the next day. In a 2000 decision, the U.S. District Court issued a restraining order against the discipline. The judge observed that "Web sites can be an early indication of a student's violent inclinations and can spread those beliefs quickly to like-minded or susceptible people. The defendant [school district], however, has presented no evidence that the mock obituaries and voting on this web site were intended to threaten anyone, did actually threaten anyone or manifested any violent tendencies whatsoever."[7] The district agreed to rescind the discipline and pay Emmett's legal fees.

The bottom line is that school districts should know that the ability to control off-campus student behavior in relation to Web sites is uncertain legal terrain. Courts will have to carefully balance the free speech rights of students against the need of school officials to maintain a safe, orderly environment free of hostility engendered by electronic sniping.

There are several alternatives for school officials frustrated by an undesirable student Web site. If the material is truly obnoxious, offensive, and insulting, but not actionable under the school district's discipline policy because of First Amendment concerns, leaders can:

- Notify parents of the infraction. Often parents are unaware of their children's activities and when notified will be grateful and immediately exercise their parental prerogative to shut down the site.

- Notify the student's Internet Service Provider. Often an ISP will have rules about what is acceptable on its system and may require that the student remove the objectionable material as a condition of continuing with Internet service.

- Wait for a private action to proceed. Sometimes when nothing is possible administratively, parties who are named or defamed on the site will seek satisfaction in the courts.

One example took place in McHenry County, Illinois, when a judge ruled on November 28, 2000, that the father of a Catholic high school student could potentially be held liable for a Web site, constructed by his son, that featured the digitally grafted picture of a female classmate's face on a hard-core sexual image. The civil lawsuit by the aggrieved girl charged the boy with several wrongful acts but also included the father in an accusation of negligence for failure to more closely supervise the teen's activities. The Judge determined that the negligence action could proceed—perhaps all the way to trial. Seeking to hold parents accountable for the actions of minor children is becoming a more frequently seen cause of action.

- Contact law enforcement if the matter is serious enough since some criminal statutes have been modified or construed by courts to cover electronic mayhem.

The problem of off-campus hate sites on the Web is likely to continue to get worse as students learn, as part of their general education at school, how to create and manipulate Web sites. Through increasing techno-literacy, students will also grow cleverer in their ability to engage in electronic rebellions.

Legal Issues Surrounding School District Internet Sites

Publishing Student Work or Pictures on the Web: Is It a Good Idea?

One of the more difficult issues for schools is how to deal with displaying student work on Web sites. While students, faculty, and parents are rightfully proud of student achievement, placing artwork, writing, or other student creations on a universally accessible electronic site is problematic and could lead to legal consequences unless school districts implement some basic precautions.

There can be benefits derived from posting student work on the school or district's Web site. It can facilitate family involvement. Friends, relatives, and the students themselves can see concrete evidence of progress and prowess. Further, the school or district Web site provides one more medium for publication, which may motivate some students—giving them another goal to strive for and another plaudit to include on resumes or in a biography of accomplishments. Some aspiring high school students, for instance, want their work displayed electronically because they can easily refer colleges to the site to see a portfolio displaying their abilities.

Should a school district place pictures of students or student work on its Web site?

- Photographs of students should not be displayed on a school building Web site or districtwide Web site unless prior, explicit permission has been obtained from a parent or guardian.

- People may view the Internet differently than a standard paper publication. It is more likely that someone outside the school community will intentionally access computerized information—given its easy electronic retrieval—rather than intentionally seek out a paper document. Include a clause about Internet use and have a separate Internet release in the district's acceptable use policy.

- Unauthorized use of a student's likeness or other identifiable information could constitute a violation of the Family Educational Rights and Privacy Act (FERPA).

The disadvantages are equally apparent. Individuals with bad intentions can use information they obtain—names, interests, location—to harm vulnerable individuals. While the prospects are probably remote for school or district liability when someone obtains from a school-sponsored Web site information used in an unlawful or harmful activity, schools could potentially be held responsible.

Web Publishing Policies

To maximize the benefits of displaying student material on school Web sites while minimizing the risks, create a Web publishing policy that requires explicit parental

permission—through a signed release—for the school or the district to display the student's work on its Web site. This should be a stand-alone release, not to be confused with the more common release that allows photographs of students to be taken and "published." In addition, districts must decide if a one-time release will suffice or if it is necessary to obtain permission each time a work is considered for the site.

Another approach is to create an omnibus release for parents to sign at the beginning of the year. Such a policy would include a checklist of possible types of information, images, and media—such as voice, likeness, quotes, written material, and graphic or other artwork. Parents or guardians choose the categories of media and information that are acceptable to them.

While parental releases can lessen the likelihood of liability for schools, caution should be the watchword in school and district Web publishing policies, with student safety as the guiding principle. There are a number of safeguards districts can implement to protect students. In Eugene, Oregon, for example, the school district's policy requires that only the first names of students can be published, that pictures of students not be accompanied by identifying information, and that students' home addresses and telephone numbers never be posted.

Sample Web Publishing Statement
Preamble

It is clear that there are significant risks, as well as significant advantages, involved with allowing students to be identified on the Internet. Therefore, students should not be easily identifiable from materials they might publish on the Internet. No directory information should be posted on the Web for students whose parents have returned the form asking that such information not be released.

Guidelines:

- Only first names will be used in published student work.
- Pictures that are a part of student publishing should not include identifying information.
- Under no circumstances should a student's home address or phone number be included.
- If replies to published student work are appropriate, the sponsoring teacher's address should be the e-mail address displayed, not the student's.
- In special circumstances with parent-signed release, identifying information can be added.

— Lane County School District No. 4J, Eugene, Oregon, 4J Student Internet Privacy Guidelines

In addition to protecting students, this policy could help school officials and teachers involved in a court proceeding to make the case that the district acted reasonably considering both the circumstances and the risk. Schools should also be cautious about identifying a teacher with specific students, allowing student work to lie dormant on the Web site, or creating URLs that inadvertently give Web-savvy wrongdoers access to a student's full first and last name. Also, attorneys and school officials should look at the totality of the Web site, realizing that disparate pieces of information scattered among different locations can be cobbled together to create an informative profile of an individual student.

One other privacy-related consideration is worth pondering when deciding what kinds of student information or material to post and how to display it. The Individuals with Disabilities Education Act (IDEA) prohibits districts from disclosing to unauthorized persons or entities any information about a student's disability. Under some interpretations, if a picture reveals a student's disability, the district should obtain a parent's written consent. The Missouri School Boards Association provided the following example in a discussion of Internet-related legal issues: When a picture of the special education teacher of the year appears in the local newspaper with the teacher's students, it immediately identifies those students as special needs students and could violate IDEA.[8]

Schools should be especially careful about allowing staff to create class-specific Web sites, school-specific sites, or other stand-alone presentations. Consider whether to either (1) forbid the practice and require instead that all submissions be located on the districtwide Web site; or (2) establish a rigorous pre-clearance requirement that allows a responsible official to screen and approve possible submissions.

Potential Liability in Linking to Other Web Sites

Links supply another source of potential liability for school districts. For example, a parent and/or student could sue the school system for injuries caused by information received from a site, such as a site advocating racial bigotry, accessed through a link found on a school-sponsored Web page. It would admittedly be difficult for a plaintiff to meet the burden of proof necessary to hold the school district responsible for whatever harm befell him or her. The plaintiff would need to convince a judge that the school district was embracing or promoting such ideas. While the risk of losing a case of this type is slight, the situation could certainly cause the district embarrassment.

There is a provision in the Communications Decency Act[9] that appears to be a "safe harbor" against such lawsuits for Internet service providers, which includes school districts. Nevertheless, to avoid problems, districts should scrupulously research all proposed links to make sure they do not connect users to objectionable material.

A common practice followed by many Web sites, both school and non-school, is posting a disclaimer. The following statement provides sample language for a disclaimer.

Links to Third Party Sites

The links in this area will let you leave the school district site. The linked sites are not under the control of the district, and the district is not responsible for the contents of any linked site or any link contained in a linked site, or any changes or updates to such sites. The district is providing these links to you only as a convenience, and the inclusion of any link does not imply endorsement of the site by the district.

A school district could also be sued on constitutional grounds for either allowing or prohibiting the placement of a link on a school-sponsored Web site. For example, if a student—while doing schoolwork or participating in an extracurricular activity—

wanted to create a link from a school district Web site to a site containing material promoting religious indoctrination, the district could face either: (1) a lawsuit claiming violation of the separation of church and state doctrine under the U.S. Constitution, if the district allowed the link; or (2) a lawsuit from the student alleging a violation of his or her freedom of religion and freedom of speech if the district refused to permit the link.

Controlling Web Site Content

School Web site content remains largely a new frontier issue; therefore, no case law is available on the subject. But it seems likely that courts would treat a district-sponsored Web site in much the same way it would treat a school newspaper, theatrical production, or other expressive activity that one might reasonably consider to be sanctioned by the school and school district.

FREE EXPRESSION

Can racist political speech be linked to the school's Web site?

Local racist John Doe is running for the school board. He places information on the school district Web site and proceeds to engage in a political debate about the school board election, decry the shameful information being taught in the district's schools, and make scurrilous remarks about the abilities of various school employees. Now what?

Can religious groups have their link?

The Generica High School Rally 'Round the Flagpole Club (Christian prayer group) begins posting material on the school Web site. It turns out to be one of the most visited connections to the Web site—not because of its religious content, but because of its "Sinner of the Week" column. Club members vote on which teacher or student was the biggest sinner during the previous week, write about which Commandment was broken, and give details on the actions that the sinner took in breaking the Commandment. Any problem with the district prohibiting this practice?

Answer: If the Web site is an open forum for expression, it's the cyber-age equivalent of a soap box in a park. Therefore, everyone is entitled to a say. Since schools must be neutral toward religion, they may not restrict their own prayer club from posting information on the Web site. (See Board of Westside Community Schools v. Mergens, 109 S.Ct. 3240 (1990)). The school district can, however, declare the site a closed forum and squelch all voices but its own.

The U.S. Supreme Court has held in *Hazelwood School District v. Kuhlmeier*[10] that "educators do not offend the First Amendment by exercising editorial control over the style and content of student speech in school-sponsored expressive activities, so long as their actions are reasonably related to 'legitimate pedagogical concerns.'" In other words, a school may prohibit expressive activity that is, for example, ungrammatical, poorly written, inadequately researched, biased or prejudiced, vulgar or profane, or unsuitable for immature audiences.[11]

FREE EXPRESSION

Can a student create a private Web site disparaging school & teachers?

A group of enterprising students at Fallacy High School create their own Web site without using any school district technology. The Web server for their site is a private Web server. They call their site the "Fallacy High Hi-Times." On their Web site, students post articles favoring the legalization of illicit drugs and euthanasia of teachers over the age of 30. And they write disparaging articles about Fallacy High School, the Fallacy administration, the Fallacy faculty, and student leaders at school. People logging onto the Web site could believe it is a Fallacy High School-sponsored Web site because of the name. Does the school have any leverage in preventing publication of this Web site and material?

Answer: This is an emerging area of the law. It is unsettled as to whether school districts have the right to discipline students who do not use school-owned technology and yet engage in speech that is potentially disruptive to the school community. Incidents of this type that have flared up in various parts of the country have been met with mixed success by school districts and mixed answers by the courts.

Perhaps the best way to assure courts treat Web sites in the same manner as other school-sponsored publications is to include the subject within the acceptable use policy. For example:

Web Pages

All Web pages created by students and student organizations on the district's computer system will be subject to treatment as district-sponsored publications. Accordingly, the district reserves the right to exercise editorial control over such publications.

School board members, religious student groups, or others with a strong agenda may seek access to the school's Web site. School boards should carefully consider what standards and rules apply in granting access to district Web sites. In addition to general guidelines, some school districts accomplish the task with academic requirements. They can demand that any student work published on the Web meet standards of spelling, grammar, adequate research, or other qualitative measures.

In a decision that is believed to be the first of its kind, and which might be helpful to schools, a New York judge ruled that the time limit for liability in connection with work published on Web sites is finite. At issue was a one-year statute of limitations in New York state and the question of whether the libel clock starts to run on the first day the article is published, or whether it is re-set to zero each day the offending work appears because it is "re-published." The judge in the Court of Claims applied the single publication rule, saying that just because information continues to exist in cyberspace is no reason to consider it as being published each day.[12]

Making an analogy to traditional paper publications, the judge noted that newspapers, magazines, and books can be published on a single day; sit around for days, months, or years afterward; and then be picked up and read by anyone with access. The judge

FREE EXPRESSION

Who governs electronic newspapers on the school district's Web site?

Nostalgia High has an open guest book for people to share what they think of the school programs and Web site. The school district invites community participation via the site's chat rooms, guest book, and bulletin boards. The school board has proclaimed that it wants the district's Web site to be as open for expression as a school board meeting. School board members welcome input on the Web site regarding curriculum, important political issues regarding education, and anything that the community considers important in relation to education.

Sophomore Judy Java prints an underground newspaper and distributes it at school. She enjoys criticizing various things about the school, using four-letter words and publishing questionable stories and poetry that include vulgar language. Since Judy produces the paper at home, she might actually have a legal right to distribute the paper on campus.

No one pays attention to Judy anymore. She therefore posts her newsletter on the district Web site bulletin board. To make sure people pay attention, she now writes shameful articles about which teachers are drunks and have driving under the influence (DUI) charges now or in the past. She makes allegations about which teachers cheat on their spouses, with whom and when, and about which teachers have made inappropriate advances to students. Judy's articles are widely read and have popularized the district Web site considerably. Judy is even dreaming of a career with one of the Hollywood gossip tabloids. May the district keep Judy off its Web site?

Answer: Under First Amendment freedom of expression law, when a school opens a forum (like the Web site in this scenario) to unrestricted public expression, it has difficulty thereafter controlling the content and who has access to that forum. Nostalgia High has opened its Web site to the community to discuss its schools. Judy can argue that she is discussing the community schools by revealing which teachers are fit examples for youth. With an open forum Web site, a court would probably allow Judy to continue her underground link to the school's Web site. (See Beussink v. Woodland R-IV School District, 1:98CV93 RWS; U.S. District Court for the Eastern District of Missouri. In December 1998, the court issued a temporary injunction against the school district's 10-day suspension of a student who created a private Web site containing material critical of the school. The student linked the offending site to the district's site.)

Policy Solution: The school could eliminate expression such as Judy's in two main ways: (1) It could prevent the Web site from being used as a community forum for discussion of education issues; or (2) It could adopt a Web site policy that designates the Web site as a "closed forum," for district use only, to transmit information to the public. However, neither solution would address the unresolved issue of a student creating on a home computer a Web site that includes disparaging comments about the school or its people and linking that site to the school's official site.

found the Web site material to be comparable. For school publishers, this decision, in concert with a state statute of limitations, could provide an effective defense against a tardy libel claim.

Student Use of E-mail and Other Electronic Exchange Formats

Many schools allow students to have e-mail addresses, but e-mail creates its own unique set of issues because of the swiftness of communication. Even with appropriate supervision, a student can quickly create havoc through immature and improper use of the technology. For example, in Marshfield, Massachusetts, several United States

LIABILITY

Are schools responsible if a student uses school Internet access to learn how to build bombs—then uses that newly acquired skill?

Johnny is a very smart and inquisitive seventh grader who has no Internet access at home. His teacher has just taught him how to use the Internet to find information about different subjects, such as the gross national product of South American countries and the yearly rainfall in the Congo, both of which are topics Johnny is supposed to be studying in class. Johnny is more interested in other things and spends hours on the Internet learning how to make letter bombs and pipe bombs. No one notices what Johnny is up to until he blows up the local convenience store across the street from the school.

The store owner sues the school; furthermore, Johnny's parents demand copies of all e-mail Johnny has sent over the school's e-mail system. Is the school liable? Must the school turn over the e-mail?

Answer: If a jury felt that the school district's supervision of Johnny's Internet access was inadequate, the school district might be liable. The student acceptable use agreement can include "hold harmless" language that seeks to waive liability—so that neither the parent, guardian, nor student signing it could sue. Here, however, the store owner is a third party not involved in the agreement. The student acceptable use policy does not extend to that person.

As to the e-mail, in consenting to terms of the acceptable use agreement, Johnny and his parent would have waived certain privacy rights, including giving the school permission to monitor his e-mail. In this context, schools might be compelled to relinquish the e-mail during discovery (the question and answer phase of litigation—before trial—when attorneys are compelled to give information to the other side).

Policy Solution: Policies will not prevent liability to third parties such as the convenience store owner. But vigilant supervision of student use of the Internet should, in theory, catch such errant misbehavior. Students browsing bomb-making sites could be subject to school discipline for unauthorized use. Alternatively, schools and teachers can argue to a court that they took reasonable steps to prevent students from acquiring knowledge that could be used to harm people.

Secret Service agents quickly arrived on a school's doorstep with grim expressions and multiple questions after a student prankster sent a death threat to former President Clinton via the White House Web site. Worse yet, the threat was signed with the name of the school principal.

In February 1999, a high school in Raritan Township, New Jersey had a similar experience. A 17-year-old student was charged with harassment after he sent a threatening message to the president. The student, who was in the school's computer lab, was supposed to be working on a science research project.

In another recent incident, a student e-mailed a bomb threat to a major national newspaper, costing the threatened organization time, money, and fear while extraordinary precautions were taken. The message was traced back to a school district computer, but the suspected student initially denied any involvement. The computer's log was precise about the time and message. Both the student's home state and the state in which the newspaper was based considered filing criminal charges. The student quickly confessed and wrote a letter of apology to those whom he had inconvenienced.

The key challenge for schools is to balance the hazards against the potential good that can come from allowing students access to e-mail and Internet tools. The benefits include having electronic "pen pals," performing research, establishing communications with professionals in key occupations, and growing familiar with the "world's largest library," the World Wide Web. Classrooms can connect with others from across the country and around the globe, using Internet technology and school profiles to find just the right match. One of the largest such online communities, e-PALS Classroom Exchange (http://www.epals.com/index.html), has more than 11,500 classrooms registered, representing 850,000 students in more than 90 countries, and provides information on each class's ages, grade level, language, study projects, and other relevant data.

Beyond e-mail, there are the more interactive forms of communication, such bulletin boards or electronic mailing lists or e-mail groups, which provide a venue for people who have similar interests and want to share ideas about a particular topic. Public chat rooms are live, real-time electronic conversations conducted by two or more people who transmit messages typed on keyboards to a central bulletin board, where everyone "in the room" can read them. A variation is a private chat, during which two or more people retire to a secluded "electronic space" to chat.

The interactive chat feature has many educational benefits. In 1997, some students followed a group of space shuttle astronauts as they prepared for their mission, conducting live chats with them to get first-hand information. The downside of chat rooms is that it is difficult to restrict what information students receive or disclose about themselves during the chat session.

Monitoring Student E-mail

At the beginning of the school year, or whenever a new e-mail account is established, school personnel should obtain written permission from both the student and the student's parent or guardian to monitor electronic mail. Intercepting students' e-mail without such permission may place schools in conflict with The Electronic

Communications Privacy Act (ECPA)[13], which makes it a criminal offense to intercept e-mail while it is in transit. However, the Act does not make it unlawful to intercept electronic communication if at least one party to the communication has given his or her consent to the interception (See *Bohach v. City of Reno*[14], which found that the city is permitted to read stored electronic messages without violating ECPA).

Electronic Communications Privacy Act

The E-mail Permission Exception, 18 U.S.C. 62510-2520

It shall not be unlawful under this chapter for a person not acting under color of law* to intercept a wire, oral, or electronic communication where such person is a party to the communication or where one of the parties to the communication has given prior consent to such interception unless such communication is intercepted for the purpose of committing any criminal or tortious act in violation of the Constitution or laws of the United States or of any State.

*This phrase refers to an actual legal right or the appearance of one. It encompasses not only acts done by state officials (including school officials) within the limits of their lawful authority, but also acts done beyond the bounds of lawful authority and made possible only because the wrongdoer is cloaked with the authority of the state.

Even when a student has not returned a consent form, there is some indication that courts will take a lenient view, allowing school districts to view students' electronic mail stored on the district's computer. In *Steve Jackson Games, Inc. v. U.S. Secret Service*[15], the federal court interpreted the Act as not applying to information stored on the provider's system.

Some school districts, operating on attorney advice, decide that in lieu of a student permission slip, they will simply notify parents annually of the risks involved in using education technology. There are several reasons underlying this approach. First, if the school board believes that the Internet is an important educational tool, then all students should have access to it, not just students who have returned consent forms. Also, as the

Student e-mail should never be considered private

- E-mail is not a confidential medium for transmitting personal messages.
- E-mail can be reviewed by others and should be used only for legitimate educational purposes or as authorized.
- E-mail should be viewed by students as the sending of a written memorandum by electronic means.
- Students should be informed that their e-mail will be monitored and the discipline policy enforced if infractions occur.
- There is no guarantee of privacy when using any school technology.
- Students should be advised not to give personal information over the Internet.

Internet becomes more integral to school curricula, it will become increasingly difficult for students who do not return the forms to academically progress with other students. Also, no permission system is fail-safe. If a student without a form gains access to inappropriate material, general use of that very form could enhance liability.

A combined approach may be productive for some schools. A permission slip is particularly effective when students have an individual account to which they have remote access from home or some other location. If the only time that a student would have school-related access to the Internet is in the classroom or library, under adult supervision, then perhaps only parental notification is necessary.

Some school districts may encounter special problems if they use an outside network to supply Internet access and e-mail capability. This arrangement is especially popular in rural school districts and those with limited resources because the cost is low. These districts should consider whether the Internet provider is willing to allow officials access to tracking mechanisms when the need arises and under what circumstances the two parties might be working at cross purposes. Provisions should be included in the initial contract or as an amendment by mutual consent.

Some school districts decide not to give students e-mail accounts but to grant the privilege to teachers and let classroom leaders decide when students need to use electronic means to facilitate learning. Still other districts create "project accounts" that have starting and ending dates; the user name reflects the project rather than a person. Whatever the technique, the same precautions about permission, supervision, and acceptable use standards still apply.

Filtering, Monitoring, and Blocking Access to the Internet

The idea of installing filters to block school networks from access to certain Internet sites that contain objectionable material has been controversial. But passage of the Children's Internet Protection Act (CIPA) in Congress in late 2000 made it mandatory as a condition of receiving Education-rate, or E-rate, funds. The E-rate program requires telecommunications companies by law to offer discount prices to schools on Internet access, internal connections, and other electronic infrastructure.

Giving school districts wide discretion, CIPA requires school districts to adopt an Internet safety plan that, among other things, addresses:

- access by minors to inappropriate material on the Internet and World Wide Web

- safety and security of minors with regard to e-mail, chat rooms, and other forms of direct electronic communication

- unauthorized online access by minors, including "hacking" and other unlawful activities

- unauthorized disclosure, use, and dissemination of personal information

The law applies to both public schools and municipal libraries. In 2001, it was challenged as unconstitutional by library groups and the American Civil Liberties Union. However, the only clauses at issue in the case dealt exclusively with libraries, and a settlement provides libraries with an additional year to comply.

Three types of software give school districts some control over what Internet content is accessible on their networks. **Blocking** software prohibits users from gaining access to certain sites. **Filtering** software, identifies objectionable words and phrases and blocks access to sites that contain them. **Inclusion** software allows access **only** to designated sites. A fourth type, **Monitoring** software, is the equivalent of an alert after-the-fact. It reviews data packets to detect when students might have accessed inappropriate Web sites and notifies the monitors. Because it does not prevent students from going to objectionable sites, it is unclear whether the monitoring software would meet the requirements of CIPA although regulations accompanying the law leave school officials a wide berth.

The first three mechanisms discussed above are dependent on the software program's thoroughness and adaptability to change, and all have weaknesses. For example, a program could screen out sites of potential educational value (such as one about breast cancer) because it searches mechanically for words that seem suggestive or inappropriate. And filtering software might ban student access to information about the Mars exploration project on NASA's Web site because the URL, *http://rsd.gsfc.nasa.gov/marslife/marsexpl.htm*, contains the letters "s-e-x."

Besides the issue of protecting students from objectionable material, issues of free speech and censorship often take center stage in deciding whether to implement filtering technology. Some argue in favor of full access to "the world's largest library" while others say filtering is a useful tool that facilitates smooth use of education technology resources and reduces complaints of teachers, students, and others. Each community should weigh the relative merits and come up with a policy conclusion. From a legal standpoint, currently there is not a great deal more potential liability incurred with or without the filter.[16]

Sexually Explicit Material

In *Reno v. American Civil Liberties Union*,[17] the United States Supreme Court reviewed provisions of the Communications Decency Act of 1996 (CDA)[18], which imposed criminal penalties for the knowing transmission of obscene or indecent messages to any recipient under 18 years of age. Section 223(d) of the Act prohibits knowingly sending or displaying any message that, in context, depicts or describes, in terms patently offensive as measured by contemporary community standards, sexual or excretory activities or organs.

In its 1997 decision, the Court held that CDA was overly broad and violated the First Amendment of the U.S. Constitution. The High Court stated that the breadth of CDA's coverage was unprecedented and that the undefined terms "indecent" and "patently offensive" cover large amounts of non-pornographic material, material that has significant educational or other value. The Court said the CDA's prohibition might extend to discussions about safe sexual practices, artistic images that include nude subjects, and arguably, the card catalog of the Carnegie library.[19]

LIABILITY

Are schools responsible when children use school computers for live cyber-chats and become victims of in-person abuse?

Sandra is a 13-year-old middle school pupil who spends hours on the Internet at school. She has no Internet access at home, and her parents know very little about the Internet. One of her favorite pastimes is to enter electronic chat rooms and talk to others about personal things like relationships, love, and life experiences. Her teacher lets her use the Internet in the classroom every day at lunch. Sandra meets a wonderful 13-year-old boy via a chat room. He is everything that she dreamed of in a romantic relationship. She arranges to meet him at a local fast food hamburger restaurant. It turns out her chat-room friend is actually a 45-year-old child molester. Sandra is abducted and molested. Sandra and her parents sue the school for negligent supervision. Could the district and teacher be held liable?

Answer: The school district and the teacher might be held liable if a jury concluded that the teacher's supervision was not reasonable under the circumstances. One way a plaintiff could prove its case is by calling school administrators from other districts as witnesses to discuss the risks inherent on the Web and the necessity to supervise student use of the Web. This hypothetical is loosely based on a situation that occurred in San Diego. (Dailey v. Los Angeles Unified School Dist., 2 Cal.3d 741, 470 P.2d 360 (1970), which sets forth the duty of student supervision by school personnel.)

Policy Solution: Before allowing students access to the Internet, school districts should require that students and parents or guardians sign a student acceptable use agreement. By including "hold harmless" clauses and a release in that agreement, the district and teacher could argue in some states that they cannot be held legally responsible because such liability was waived. (Aaris v. Las Virgenes Unified School Dist., 64 Cal.App.4th 1112 (Cal. 1998) upholding school release language).

Sometimes, school districts choose to forego a permission slip in favor of parental notification that outlines the risks of Internet access. The belief behind that approach is that some students who have not signed a consent form may gain access to the Internet anyway. If that person reads inappropriate material, the consent form then could enhance liability since the school district did not follow its own policy. Perhaps the safest approach is to arrange for both a permission slip and parental notification.

School officials therefore should be aware that the CDA no longer applies, but political concern for an effective method of keeping sexually explicit material out of the hands of minors still remains. Several proposed laws have been initiated in Congress to put the brakes on what many representatives and senators see as runaway access to unpalatable material.

Student Privacy Concerns

Providing Internet access for students raises privacy issues. School districts have a policy choice to make about whether to review student e-mail. If they choose to do so or to reserve that option, they should clearly communicate to students and parents or guardians that students should not expect privacy when communicating by e-mail, using the Internet, or performing other work utilizing district-owned technology assets. Failure to notify students and parents properly could nullify any later attempt to see otherwise private information. This factor could be the linchpin in defending the right to search for incriminating information when enforcing the student ccceptable use policy. [See Chapter 3: *Legal Considerations in Regulating Employee Use of School Technology* for a further discussion of this topic.]

Family Educational Rights and Privacy Act

The Family Educational Rights and Privacy Act of 1974[20] (FERPA) requires districts to have a policy that grants parents the right to inspect and review the education records of their children. FERPA requires that school districts establish procedures to provide parents access to records within 45 days of a request. Educational records are defined as those records, files, documents, and other materials that contain information maintained by an education agency or institution. Regulations related to the Act's implementation clearly include stored electronic data in the definition of educational records. If a system is not in place for finding the electronic information efficiently, school officials could find themselves in the midst of the time-consuming and challenging task of locating information, as the 45-day clock ticks on a request.

FERPA also requires that schools obtain a parent's written consent before disclosing personally identifiable information about the student. Most school computers that provide Internet access automatically store information about the student's electronic activities. That data might fall within the FERPA definition of education information about students, thus entitling parents to see it. To the extent this information identifies a particular student's use of the school's Internet connection, it could qualify as personally identifiable information that must be protected. Another issue that a school district should consider is whether e-mail that is sent or received by a student on the school's e-mail system and then stored on the school's server, is an education record under FERPA, to which a parent would have right of access. The answer to this question is by no means clear at present, but some recent cases involving school technology assets are worth considering.

A recent case involving the right of parents to access records of students' Internet activities was decided in New Hampshire under that state's freedom of information act.

Family Educational Rights and Privacy Act (FERPA) — 20 U.S.C. 61232g

- When exchanging or sharing records with other school districts or public agencies, safeguards must be in place to protect the privacy rights of students under federal law.

- The same rules of confidentiality apply with respect to student records that are computerized.

The case, *James M. Knight v. School Administrative Unit #16* [21], from Exeter, New Hampshire, involves a parent who suspected that students were visiting inappropriate sites on the Web and requested that he and other parents be permitted to inspect the logs that track site visits made by students. The Rockingham County Superior Court in the State of New Hampshire agreed that the right existed under the state's "Right-to-Know" public access to records law—not ruling at all about FERPA. It is important to note that the decision is confined to New Hampshire and is not binding on any other locations. Although public information law differs from state-to-state, school officials should be aware that attorneys for probing parents may seek to use the New Hampshire decision for its persuasive value.

Thus far, FERPA questions related to videotaping students have no definitive answers. For example, if a school system has a policy of placing video cameras on all school buses and a camera captures both "innocent" students and those involved in an altercation, which results in disciplinary action, should persons other than district staff be able to view the tape?

In *Tampa Television Inc. v. School Board of Hillsborough County* [22], a three-judge Florida appeals court panel ruled unanimously that a videotape recording of students riding on Hillsborough County public school buses qualifies as "student records and reports," according to a Florida statute.[23] However, case law is unclear as to the extent of student privacy with respect to videotaping in public places, such as a schoolbus or classroom.[24]

A similar question about the use of videotapes may arise in other contexts. For example, a student videotapes a pep rally with students clearly identified and wants to

Sample Video Surveillance Policy

The Board authorizes the use of video cameras on school property and transportation vehicles to ensure the health, welfare and safety of all staff, students and visitors to district buses or property, and to safeguard district facilities and equipment. Video cameras may be used in locations deemed appropriate by the superintendent. The district has carefully weighed and balanced the privacy rights of students and staff. Authority for school officials exists as follows:

- The district shall notify its staff and students that video surveillance may occur on any school property or transportation vehicle. The district shall incorporate the notice into the handbook.

- The use of video surveillance equipment shall be supervised by the transportation supervisor or the building administrator, as applicable.

- Students or staff in violation of Board policies, administrative regulations, building rules or law shall be subject to appropriate disciplinary action. Others may be referred to law enforcement agencies.

- Video recordings may become a part of a student's educational record or a staff member's personnel record. The district shall comply with all applicable state and federal laws related to record maintenance and retention.

- Audio shall not be a part of the video recordings made, reviewed or stored by the district.

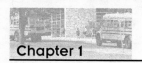

have the tape broadcast over the school's community public access channel—should that request be granted? Interpretations by well-informed attorneys vary, and it is best for a school district to consult its advisor about these issues and how best to proceed.

Equal Access

A Year 2000 survey of public schools by the U.S. Education Department's National Center for Education Statistics found that 98 percent of U.S. schools and 77 percent of all U.S. classrooms are connected to the Internet. However, home computers are less widespread. A report issued in January 2001 by the David and Lucile Packard Foundation found that merely 22 percent of children in families with annual incomes of less than $20,000 have access to a home computer. By contrast, approximately 90 percent of families with incomes of more than $75,000 have a computer at home.

It would be prudent for school districts to consciously avoid allowing situations to develop where the district staff can be justifiably accused of discriminating against certain segments of their student populations by requiring students to complete out-of-school academic requirements or assignments using technology to which they may not have access. Examples of such assignments include conducting online research or creating reports using presentation of graphing software.

Ideally, a school district's practice would permit children with disabilities to have equal access to the computers and other technologies commonly used by other students. Approaches that impose additional restrictions or prohibit use by disabled students could place a school district at risk of a lawsuit under Section 504 of the Rehabilitation Act of 1973 or Title II of the Americans with Disabilities Act (ADA), both of which forbid discrimination. Potential causes of action also include the Individuals with Disabilities Education Act (IDEA). [For more on this topic, see the ADA section of Chapter 2: *Administrative Issues in School Technology*. See also *Technology for Students with Disabilities: A Decision Maker's Resource Guide*, published in 1997 by the National School Boards Association and the U.S. Department of Education's Office of Special Programs and included in the resource section of Chapter 2.]

Safeguarding Students and Enforcing School Rules

Using Technology to Help Keep Children Safe

Innovative technologies provide diligent administrators with additional tools that can be used to keep school campuses safe and to reduce potential legal liability. In North Carolina, for instance, educators are asking students to catch the W.A.V.E.—the Working Against Violence Everywhere program of education and violence prevention. While it has been widely accepted for its laudable traits, W.A.V.E. has not won universal approval. Its most controversial feature is a Web site that allows students to provide anonymous tips about potential violence via an 800 number.[25] The program has been active since February 2000. Advocates maintain that can potentially provide early detection and, ultimately, deterrence. Such notice can mean that school officials reduce or remove liability claims that often follow after a violent act. Civil libertarians, however, are critical of the W.A.V.E. approach, believing that a system based on anonymous tips is too open to abuse and infringes upon the rights of students.

In Smithtown, New York, an administrator can use a palm-sized computer to check a student's class schedule to see whether a student who is in the hallway should really be in class. That monitoring tool can prevent confrontations between students and help to reduce liability stemming from mishaps that occur when students leave the building, without permission and unnoticed. Some school districts are experimenting with giving scanners to bus drivers so they can scan the I.D. cards of students who hop onto their bus for a ride to or from school. By doing so, school administrators can tell parents or authorities whether and precisely when a student used bus transportation.

Another electronic transportation-related device, similar to a beeper, is kept by the student and emits a sound when the bus is within one mile of the designated stop instead of having students stand on the corner not knowing when the bus will arrive. This strategy addresses some potential liability problems related to behavior in groups or students being alone.

Using Technology to Stop Academic Cheating

Smart technology permits school officials to monitor student behavior in new ways. In recent years, there has been a proliferation of "paper mills" on the Internet, providing high school and college students with ready-made or ostensibly customized research papers on a wide variety of topics. Anti-plagiarism software is a tool that some classroom teachers and school districts employ to detect students seeking to cheat using online sources. While such actions do not necessarily fall under the acceptable use policy, they are generally considered a violation of the student code of conduct and can trigger various disciplinary penalties.

Various anti-plagiarism software packages use different techniques. Some look for phrases within a student's paper that match phrases found in papers and other material contained in the program's data bank. The data banks cull material from cheat sites, encyclopedias, and other sources, and, in some cases, from student papers that were searched to detect plagiarism and stored. The programs scan the Internet and its own data for key words, highlight matching passages, and provide links to the online source so that teachers can follow-up. Still others search for matching sentences or whole documents rather than just key words. With some publishers, schools can purchase software for its own use while other companies command a per-use fee.

The anti-plagiarism approach can be highly effective in detecting those students who are trying to beat the system. But, it could result in faulty accusations. Therefore, districts should develop a strict policy, move cautiously, and also rely upon traditional investigation techniques to confirm suspicions before taking disciplinary action based solely on the software program's findings.

Commercialism Arrangements

School districts are routinely approached by commercial entities with offers designed to gain access to the district's electronic systems. For those with products or services to sell, school systems can be the targets of strategic effort to capture the attention not only of youth, but also parents and other community members who might look to schools for information.

In New York City, for instance, the board of education voted to create a separate, board-owned company to offer a Web portal and free Internet services. For a fee, businesses can become sponsors and can buy licenses to use a board of education logo in their advertising. Also, whenever a subscriber uses the service to shop online, the district receives a commission on purchases. The board anticipates that the arrangement will generate enough dollars to purchase 85,000 laptop computers, Internet devices, and other electronic gear for 8th graders each year.

A September 2000 report by the United States General Accounting Office (GAO) identified four categories of commercial activity in schools: (1) the sale of products; (2) direct advertising—for example, advertisements in school corridors or on school buildings; (3) indirect advertising—for example corporate-sponsored educational materials or teacher training; and (4) market research.[26] All four categories can potentially apply to commercial relationships in the electronic milieu.

The 45-page GAO report noted that one high school it visited had replaced its newspaper with a Web page and then sold ads on the Web page to help support the journalism program. Such an approach raises questions of propriety, access (for those students who may not have Internet access at home and few opportunities to access the paper at school), administrative investment (to solicit the ads, ensure they get placed on the site in a timely way, and collect the revenue), and other questions that defy easy answers.

Education organizations are also concerned about the phenomenon, decrying what is perceived as "commercialism" in schools, and there are organized pockets of resistance to schools entering into business relationships with for profit companies. The National Parent Teacher Association produced "Guidelines for Corporate Involvement," a series of eight principles that should be applied when considering a school-business partnership (http://www.pta.org/programs/guidelines1.htm).

The Center for Commercial-Free Public Education declares its mission to be providing "support to students, parents, teachers, and other concerned citizens organizing across the U.S. to keep their schools commercial-free and community controlled." The organization advocates four guiding principles, which are listed below:

Advertising in Electronic Media

1. Except for courses of study which have specific lessons related to advertising, students shall not be required to observe, listen to or read commercial advertising in the classroom.

2. The school district shall not enter into any contract to obtain electronic equipment or software, that will obligate the district to expose students to advertising directed at young people during school time or at home while completing school assignments.

3. The school district shall not enter into any contract to obtain electronic equipment or software that will obligate the school to post information about school procedures or events on electronic media that contain advertising directed at students.

4. The school district will not enter into any contract for electronic media services, where personal information will be collected from the students by the providers of the services in question. Personal information includes, but is not limited to, the student's name, telephone number and home address.

Resistance might also take the form of health concerns. For example, contracts with food or beverage companies could lead to objections based on promoting obesity or unhealthy eating habits. Lately, some local chapters of the American Dental Association have opposed soft drink contracts.

Guidelines for School-Business Partnerships

1. **Attorneys are crucial guides when discussing electronic access rights.**

   Although relations with the courting company may be cordial and the terms seemingly fair, the final outcome of discussions will be a contract that could bind the district for years to come. Unlike philanthropy, what is being negotiated is not a charitable contribution but a business agreement—just like with any other vendor.

   Attorneys can help with the arms-distance talks and advocate for terms that are in the best interest of the school district and the children. The attorney must also help navigate the school through the practical and regulatory limitations on such activities. There may be an array of state laws that could affect a final deal.

2. **Make certain to keep the needs of children foremost in your dealings.**

3. **Make sure to limit the time period of the contract or to reserve the option to reopen the contract under changed circumstances.**

   This is a sound practice because it establishes greater freedom for school districts to maximize economic gains in an ever-changing marketplace. It might also be the best legal path. It is questionable whether a current sitting board can bind successor boards on such matters unless a law explicitly grants that authority.

4. **Be concerned about what information the district must relinquish, particularly about children, as a condition of receiving any benefits offered.**

   Think about privacy considerations and whether a business will use the special connection to the school to engage in potentially intrusive advertising or marketing activities. Privacy is probably the foremost consideration in the area of relationships with commercial entities. A recent research study by the Annenberg Public Policy Center, found that as many as 65 percent of children are willing to part with personal information, such as buying habits or the size of their allowance, in exchange for a free gift.

5. **Be careful about making promises regarding a specific place on the district's Web site.**

   Circumstances can change, and the place reserved for commercial entities during negotiations may not exist in the future. In addition, some of the most coveted, visible spaces of a district's Web site carry value for the district in communicating its own messages.

6. **Understand that money and flexibility operate in inverse proportions.**

   For businesses, exclusivity, visibility, and certainty are precious commodities. The more money they pay, therefore, the better the bargain they will demand—meaning less flexibility in district decision making.

7. **Be prepared for criticism from some segments of the community and the possibility of legal action from either spurned competitors or disgruntled citizens who challenge either the outcome or the perceived harmful results.**

   A promise of exclusivity or dominance inevitably shuts out or disadvantages competitors. Sometimes, losing businesses file a legal challenge; charging that the board of education acted outside of its authority and contrary to its own procedures, and therefore the contract is void. Thus, school representatives should be mindful that the procedure is fair and open and not tilted toward one party above all others.

8. **Administrative issues arise in the course of brokering and executing the deals, and standards must be set.**

   School boards need to develop a district policy or practice for handling electronic opportunities. Relevant questions include whether all such relationships will be centralized or whether principals are free to broker their best deal. What level of community involvement is desired or necessary before an initiative can move forward? The policy needs to address the question of who will have the final authority on matters involving commercial entities. Many school boards delegate the responsibility to the superintendent; others leave the decision to principals.

9. **Be cognizant of and sensitive to equity issues.**

   The mission of companies is to ensure and enhance profit. Yet, income generated by relationships with commercial companies raises fundamental issues of fairness. For example, should money be directed to specific school buildings that are targeted by the companies (finders keepers)? Usually the beneficiaries of that approach are larger facilities or those in geographic areas with the most economically well-off families and, therefore, the most spending power. Or, should all income accrue to the district as a whole or be redistributed in an even fashion. If the process is centralized, what formula is used to distribute the money; and what restrictions will be placed upon it?

Virtual Schools and Legal Hurdles

An innovation currently intriguing many state and local educators is the virtual school—an electronic campus where students can take public school courses online. Already, New Mexico, Kentucky, Florida, Georgia, Massachusetts, Oregon, Ohio, and New Hampshire have programs in place that allow students to earn school credit outside of the confines of the traditional bricks and mortar structure. Currently, most online school experiments are limited to high schools.

The advantages are obvious. Virtual Schools allow a single teacher to instruct far more students than could be done in the usual setting. As a result, there is economic efficiency and access for more students to an excellent teacher; curriculum can be more standardized and centralized; and students in rural or underdeveloped areas can have heretofore unheard-of access to Advanced Placement classes and other courses that might not have been available in the past. However, the disadvantages are equally obvious—loss of personal interaction with the teacher; upending the long-standing expectations about the way schooling happens; and difficulty verifying that the student is doing the work on his own.

From a legal standpoint, it means reshaping some laws to fit a different environment. For example, most funding formulas have been historically based on per pupil attendance. Should the virtual high school student be counted in the home district, the district offering the course, or in a unique way? State laws have generally confined academic credit to those courses being offered by its state-certified teachers in its state-certified classrooms. Now, out-of-state students can take a course and may want to apply to their home state for credit.

Virtual high schools provoke several questions for policymakers. Is the online course self-paced or controlled? If it is the former, then a bright student could conceivably be finished with the curriculum far ahead of her four-walled friends. How would the student's accomplishment be impacted by the typical "seat time" minimum attendance benchmark of 180-days, for instance. How do you cope with acceptable use policies and other disciplinary circumstances? Additionally, will colleges accept virtual coursework as the equivalent of regular work?

Further, how are teachers' contracts structured—are they still under supervision by local building administrators, working part-time as virtual teachers, or do they hold a full-time position? Can K-12 teachers, like their professorial counterparts in higher education, flex hours to be on-site only for the obligatory teaching time and office hours? When teachers develop the content of online courses, who owns the copyright? There may be a need to negotiate with the teachers' collective bargaining representative about the time invested, as well as teacher performance evaluations, which could be based strictly on student scores. Also, if teachers have to reside in their districts, how might a state account for the disparity in salary from place-to-place when the job is the same? To have an effective, seamless system may call for consideration of a more broad-based national certification or specialty certification for online teachers. These issues might also lead to interstate compacts.

One way around some of the in-state problems might be to classify the virtual school as a service, not as a school at all. Then it fails to trigger many of the education requirements like psychological services, lunch, etc. Advocates say that adapting the distance learning principles of higher education to the K-12 level will be especially helpful for gifted children and students with disabilities.

Even at this early stage and with more questions than answers, entrepreneurial ventures are seeking to make in-roads. Former U.S. Department of Education Secretary William J. Bennett has created a virtual school called "K12".[27] The school currently serves students up to second grade but will expand by 2004 to offer a full academic load to students from kindergarten through 12th grade. While much of the work is done online, about 25 percent of the work in the early grades is done with the oversight of a parent. The cost of attending the school full-time would be $1,000-$1,200 a year.

Conclusion

Districts should adopt acceptable use policies (AUPs) that spell out the purposes for which students may use the school's Internet connection and other electronic resources and the penalties attached to violating the policy. No one policy fits all schools. It is important for the school district to consider its size, how computers are used in its educational program, what problems have occurred in the past, and how vigorously the finer details of the policy will be enforced.

The Internet and new digital technologies are truly remarkable educational tools. If used properly, they can enhance the learning experiences of students of all ages. Because these technologies enable such a dynamic environment, and because state and federal legislatures are constantly changing the laws that govern access to digital material there, districts must give careful and continuing thought to the use of these resources and take actions that balance protection and access.

Ronald D. Wenkart is general counsel for the Orange County Department of Education in Costa Mesa, California. He supervises a legal staff that represents 28 school districts, five community college districts, four Regional Occupational Programs, the Orange County superintendent of schools and the Orange County Board of Education. He has represented schools in the state of California since 1978.

Edwin C. Darden is senior staff attorney for the National School Boards Association and editor of this publication. He is knowledgeable about a wide range of education law topics and has taught a graduate school class on the subject.

This chapter revises and updates "School District Policies for Student Use of the Internet & Electronic Publication of Student Works," by Ronald D. Wenkart and Edwin C. Darden. In Legal Issues & Education Technology: A School Leader's Guide (1999). Alexandria, VA: National School Boards Association.

Resources

The following Web sites and print resources include guidelines on crafting acceptable use policies, as well as sample policies. Some AUPs address whole school communities; others target only students, faculty, or other specific groups. Your state school boards association and department of education may offer additional sample polices. URLs were live at the time of publication.

Critiquing Acceptable Use Policies (Dave Kinnaman, 1995)
http://www.io.com/~kinnaman/aupessay.html

Acceptable Use Policies (Armadillo – The Houston Independent
School District Web Server, 1998)
http://www.rice.edu/armadillo/acceptable.html

Acceptable Use Policies of Internet Service Providers (1994)
http://www.jmls.edu/cyber/statutes/email/policies.html

Acceptable Use Policies (Web66, the University of Minnesota, no date)
http://mustang.coled.umn.edu/Started/use/Acceptableuse.html

California School Boards Association Policy Update Service (2001)
http://www.csba.org/ps/psupdate.htm

**Intermediate Education Service District and Participating School
District Internet Policy** (no date).
http://netizen.uoregon.edu/templates/esd_policy.html

Plans and Policies for Technology in Education: A Compendium. Second Edition.
2000. Alexandria, VA: National School Boards Association.

Endnotes

1   See *Reno v. ACLU*, 521 U.S. 844 (1997).

2   393 U.S. 503 (1969).

3   478 U.S. 675 (1986).

4   484 U.S. 260 (1988).

5   *Beussink v. Woodland R-IV School District*, 30 F.Supp. 2d 1175 (E.D. Mo. 1998).

6   *J.S. v. Bethlehem Area School District*, No. 2259 C.D. 1999, 2000 Pa. Commw. LEXIS 402 (Pa. Commw. Ct. 2000).

7   *Emmett v. Kent School District No. 415*, 92 F.Supp.2d 1088 (W.D. Wash. 2000).

8   See "Internet Legal Issues," Missouri School Boards' Association,
http://www.msbanet.org/legal/internetissues.htm.

9   The U.S. Supreme Court struck down the criminal penalties section (47 U.S.C. §223[a][1][B][ii]) of the Communications Decency Act in *Reno v. American Civil Liberties Union*, 117 S.Ct. 2329 (1997). However, the "safe harbor" provision (47 U.S.C. §230[c][1]) for Internet service providers (including school districts) remains in effect.

10   484 U.S. 260, 273 (1998)

11 See *Kuhlmeier*, 484 U.S. at 271.

12 *Firth v. State of New York*, 184 Misc.2d 105, 706 N.Y.S.2d 835, 2000 N.Y. Slip Op. 20191 (Court of Claims March 8, 2000).

13 18 U.S.C. Sections 2510-2520.

14 932 F.Supp. 1232 (D. Nev. 1996)

15 36 F.3d 457 (5th Cir. 1994)

16 For more information on filters, see two books: *A Practical Guide to Internet Filters* and *Shining a Light on Filters in Libraries*, both by Karen G. Schneider, MSLIS. Schneider managed "The Internet Filter Assessment Project," a librarian project, from April to September 1997. The purpose was to take a hard look at Internet content filters from a librarian's point of view. More than 40 librarians from around the world participated. Some were filter proponents, and some were not. *See* http://www.bluehighways.com/tifap

17 117 S.Ct 2329 (1997)

18 47 U.S section 223(a)(1)(B)(ii)

19 117 S.Ct 2329 (1997)

20 20 U.S.C. Section 1232(g)

21 Rockingham County (NH) Superior Court, Docket # 00C-307.

22 659 So.2d 331 (Fla. App. 2 District 1995)

23 Section 228.093(2)(e), Florida Statutes (1993), defines records as follows: "Records" and "reports" mean any and all official records, files, and data directly related to pupils and students which are created, maintained, and used by public educational institutions, including all material that is incorporated into each pupil's or student's cumulative record folder and intended for school use or to be available to parties outside the school or school system for legitimate educational or research purposes. Materials which shall be considered as part of a pupil's or student's record include, but are not necessarily limited to: identifying data, including a student's social security number; academic work completed; level of achievement records, including grades and standardized achievement test scores; attendance data; scores on standardized intelligence, aptitude, and psychological tests; interest inventory results; health data; family background information; teacher or counselor ratings and observations; verified reports of serious or recurrent behavior patterns; and any other evidence, knowledge, or information recorded in any medium, including, but not limited to, handwriting, typewriting, print, magnetic tapes, film, microfilm, and microfiche, and maintained and used by an educational agency or institution or by a person acting for such agency or institution."

24 In *M.R. v. Lincolnwood Board of Education*, 843 F.Supp., 1236 (N.D. ILL. 1994) the federal district court held that it was permissable for a school district to videotape a student's classroom behavior for evidence in a due process hearing.

25 www.waveamerica.com.

26 "Public Education: Commercial Activities in Schools." U.S. General Accounting Office, GAO/HEHS-00-156, September 8, 2000 www.gao.gov

27 www.k12.com

Chapter 2

Administrative Issues in School Technology

R. Craig Wood, Esq.
McGuireWoods LLP
Charlottesville, Virginia

Introduction

Computer technology is revolutionizing the workplace and, therefore, necessarily the public schools. The five occupations projected to grow fastest between 1998 and 2008 are computer-related, increasing at a projected rate of 27 percent, which translates into well over 5 million new jobs in ten years.[1] Likewise, research and experience suggest that when technology is used effectively in education, it can positively enhance students' educational achievement and skills acquisition.

Along with the benefits of technology in schools, however, comes a host of legal and practical implications for school boards and administrators. This chapter addresses school district liabilities in such matters as sexual harassment and universal access for individuals with disabilities. It sorts out issues with e-mail and the very real possibility that school employees will be forced to turn incriminating information over to the other side during a court case. The chapter also addresses attorney-client privilege in electronic communications and the obligation of school board members to restrain from inadvertently violating their state's open meetings law while taking advantage of the ease and convenience of electronic communications.

School District Liability for Electronic Communications

More than 40 million users send 60 billion e-mail messages a year. Students and teachers are increasingly proficient in using e-mail and often rely on it as a primary means of communication. At its best in the education field, e-mail provides a forum for students and teachers to interact and exchange academic-related ideas. At worst, e-mail can be a costly waste of human resources and a tool of harassment and discrimination.

The increased use of communications technology by administrators, teachers, and students exposes school districts to potential legal liability and practical difficulties in a number of ways. Many existing claims, such as sexual harassment, wrongful discharge, and discrimination take on a new light when the computer is the medium for the wrongful behavior or when electronic communications are used as evidence.

Sexual Harassment

E-mail no longer consists of text alone. Users now have the capability of sending and opening attachments with pictures and voice recordings. Unfortunately, some users send unsuspecting readers attachments containing suggestive pictures or obscene recordings. For example, an administrator might send a sexually explicit e-mail joke or attached picture to an unsuspecting teacher. Without appropriate safeguards, a school district could be held liable for such actions.

A sexually hostile work environment claim may arise from conduct that has the purpose or effect of unreasonably interfering with an individual's work performance or creating an intimidating, hostile, or offensive work environment.[2] Under Title VII of the Civil Rights Act of 1964, even verbal or written conduct can give rise to a "hostile environment" claim if it is sufficiently severe and pervasive to alter an employee's working conditions.

The inquiry in these types of claims often focuses on what type of improper behavior constitutes severe and pervasive conduct. In *Harley v. Coach*,[3] a racial harassment case that is analyzed under the same rules as sexual harassment cases, the court addressed this issue. The court held that one e-mail containing a racial epithet, a racial slur uttered by a supervisor, and teasing by a co-employee, were not sufficient to create a racially hostile work environment. The court relied on a Third Circuit Court of Appeals opinion, *Drinkwater v. Union Carbide Corp.*,[4] holding, "the comments . . . are not sufficient in and of themselves to support a hostile environment claim. Hostile environment harassment claims must demonstrate a continuous period of harassment, and two comments do not create such an atmosphere." These cases indicate that in some instances occasional, sporadic use of inappropriate e-mail may not constitute sexual harassment. However, it is within a court's power to find sexual harassment where it deems the conduct sufficiently egregious. Therefore, schools must institute strong policies against sexual harassment to prevent improper conduct, including in electronic communications, and take adequate remedial measures when it does occur.

Persistent offensive e-mails by (1) an administrator to a teacher; (2) a teacher to another teacher; (3) a teacher to a student; or (4) a student to a student can support a hostile environment claim,[5] and the standard of liability that applies in each case varies. The standard for finding a school liable for sexual harassment by its employees differs depending on whether the victim is an employee or a student.

Where a teacher or staff member alleges that an administrator is the harasser, vicarious liability principles apply. In other words, the school district may be held legally responsible for a hostile environment created by a supervisor with authority over the employee.[6]

An employer may escape paying money damages only where two elements are present: (1) evidence the employer exercised reasonable care to prevent and promptly correct sexually harassing behavior and (2) evidence the employee failed to take advantage of corrective opportunities available to the employee.[7] This standard is fairly strict, and unless schools take strong preventive measures they may not be able to prevent future liability. Schools must take special care in hiring and monitoring supervisors; implement a clear, specific and comprehensive sexual harassment policy with well-defined complaint procedures; disseminate and periodically review the policy with all employees; and investigate and remedy all complaints of inappropriate conduct.

The legal standard changes somewhat where a teacher sexually harasses a student. The United States Supreme Court has held that a school district may be held liable for money damages under Title IX for a teacher's sexual harassment of a student.[8] The Supreme Court ruled in *Gebser v. Lago Vista Ind. Sch. Dist.*,[9] however, that the school district may be held liable only if a school district official with authority to institute corrective measures on the district's behalf has actual notice of, and is deliberately indifferent to, the teacher's misconduct.

The Supreme Court decided the issue of student peer sexual harassment in *Davis v. Monroe County Board of Education*,[10]. The Court held that a private damages remedy can be levied against a recipient of Title IX funding, but only where the plaintiff can show the school officials acted with deliberate indifference to known acts of harassment, and that the harassment was so severe and pervasive that it constructively barred the plaintiff's access to an educational benefit or opportunity. This stringent standard makes recovery difficult, but school officials are advised to take appropriate remedial action to prevent serious claims.

While a court may find that a school district is not legally responsible for sexual harassment by a student or teacher, deterring offensive conduct is cheaper and more productive than defending a lawsuit. Adopting an e-mail and Internet policy helps to provide an affirmative defense for a school district being sued in a sexual harassment case. Under such a policy, all users should be required to review and sign an acceptable use policy statement that prohibits online sexual harassment and indicates agreement to comply with its provisions. If a district becomes aware of the sexual harassment of a student or teacher via e-mail, the district must take immediate steps to halt the harassment, including limiting the offender's use of e-mail privileges, or risk being held liable for sexual harassment. Similarly, if a teacher or administrator becomes aware of a student's misuse of e-mail privileges, those privileges should be restricted or terminated. As a further measure to deter sexual harassment suits related to e-mail misuse, a district should issue guidelines for reporting e-mail misuse.

Discrimination Claims

Just as e-mail may be a tool for sexual harassers, it may also provide fertile ground for discrimination claims ranging from age and disability discrimination to racial and gender discrimination.[11] For example, a teacher may use e-mail to send racially offensive jokes to other teachers. Or an administrator may send offensive e-mails relating to the termination of an employee, providing ammunition for a later age discrimination or disability discrimination claim. Such electronic communications could form the primary evidence in a discrimination case.

School districts should think carefully about access issues and potential claims of differential treatment by students or employees. An equitable approach to technology in the school district should allow schools to shake off adverse litigation at an early stage.

Use of E-mail in Litigation

Parties entrenched in litigation or facing potential litigation have an ongoing duty to preserve information they know is going to be relevant. E-mail, then, creates a tremendous amount of information that a district might then be obliged to disclose to the opposing side during the "discovery" phase of litigation.

During the discovery period, one side digs for information from its opponent by asking written questions and conducting face-to-face interviews. Attorneys are bound by ethics and law to turn over the requested information, even if it is incriminating or harmful to their case.

In modern litigation, attorneys frequently demand the production of relevant e-mail. Because of its informal nature, attorneys consider e-mail an excellent source of discovery and potential evidence for use at trial. Frequently, administrators and teachers make statements on e-mail that would not be placed into written memos or documents.

Although case law on e-mail as evidence in employment litigation is somewhat sparse, employers can look for increased use of e-mail as primary evidence in sexual and racial harassment cases. In *Knox v. Indiana*,[12] for example, a state employee sued for sexual harassment based in large part on e-mail messages sent to her by her supervisor. The supervisor's messages propositioned the plaintiff for sex, and the plaintiff's investigator discovered those e-mails. The United States Court of Appeals for the Seventh Circuit affirmed a jury verdict for the employee based on her Title VII claims.[13] Moreover, with the increased ability to attach pornographic images to e-mail messages, employers likely will see more sexual harassment suits by employees who are exposed to the display of pornographic or other offensive material via e-mail.

Discovery of Electronic Communications

E-mail messages are now as easily discoverable as paper messages have always been. Federal discovery rules provide that the word "document" includes electronic "data compilations,"[14] and courts interpreting the Federal Rules of Civil Procedure have held that e-mails are subject to the same discovery rules as documents.[15] Courts have also punished employers for deleting e-mails, after the initiation of litigation, that might have been useful to the adverse party at trial.[16]

To prevent the use of e-mail technology in ways that could be adverse to school districts in litigation, districts should institute e-mail use policies and uniformly enforce e-mail use restrictions. First, a policy prohibiting or severely limiting personal use of e-mail should be implemented to deter improper use and help shield a district from liability relating to such use.

Second, a district should develop a policy regarding preservation of e-mail files. Some government agencies do not back-up e-mails at all to avoid inadvertent retention problems. Whatever a school district's policy, it should be adhered to at all times, including upon request for discovery of e-mails. If a district's policy is to delete e-mail files every month, it may not deviate from that policy to defeat discovery by deleting every week. Moreover, once a discovery request has been made, school districts have a duty to refrain from deleting e-mails even if it would normally do so under its own policy. Having a fairly short time frame for e-mail retention is advisable in terms of discovery or liability. E-mail users can be encouraged to print out and save paper copies of documents important to them. Anything of great significance is then committed to paper or recalled through the memory of witnesses.

Courts have not extended a sympathetic ear to arguments of undue expense and burden in the context of discovery and demand for e-mail production. Thus, having a policy and a systematic way of proceeding on such matters avoids the potentially cumbersome and expensive process of finding an e-mail on demand. In one Ohio case, for example, a federal district court refused to grant relief to a plaintiff who asserted that such a request would require a search of 2.8 million documents, cost more than $80,000, and require hundreds of hours. The court said the request for relevant documents was reasonable and the burden was the result of the party's own unwieldy recordkeeping system. Further, the court said: When a party chooses electronic storage for information, the need for retrieval is an "ordinary and foreseeable risk."

Ways to prepare for e-mail discovery in litigation

1. Create and enforce an electronic document policy that minimizes the amount of time the information is stored.

2. Enforce the policy in a uniform way. Do not deviate when faced with litigation or potential litigation.

3. When working with the school attorney, create a litigation response that includes a process for preserving relevant data at the outset of litigation.

4. Do a litigation risk assessment that identifies weaknesses and strengths and potential high-cost areas.

5. Educate employees and emphasize the need for a business approach to e-mail communications.

6. For safety's sake, both the attorney and client should assume that their e-mail will have to be produced in discovery. Thus, unusually sensitive communications should not take place via this medium.

The duty imposed on entities to preserve e-mail was illustrated in a case involving Proctor & Gamble (P&G) and Amway[17], fierce competitors in the personal care and home care market. In the midst of a lawsuit, P&G served Amway with broad discovery documents that demanded access to e-mail correspondence. The problem was, P&G failed to retain its own e-mail files for Amway's discovery purposes. The court, illustrating the point that the practice was unacceptable, forced P&G to pay Amway $10,000, saying P&G's routine practice of purging its e-mail daily (because of the pending lawsuit) was a violation of the federal rules of discovery.

Security Issues

Because the attorney-client privilege is based in part on the expectation of privacy in communications, the increasing use of technology raises concerns about privileged communications. Generally, the attorney-client privilege extends to (1) a communication from a client (2) to the client's lawyer or the lawyer's agent (3) relating to the lawyer's rendering of legal advice (4) made with the expectation of confidentiality and (5) not in furtherance of a future crime or tort, provided the privilege has not been waived.

The fourth element, an expectation of confidentiality, has particular relevance to e-mail correspondence. If the client does not treat the information as confidential, the client will not have an expectation of privacy, and the privilege may never arise. In *Bowne of New York City, Inc. v. AmBase Corp.*,[18] the court held that the disclosure of attorney confidences to corporate employees for purposes unrelated to the obtaining of legal services from the corporation's attorneys vitiates the privilege. It warned, "[I]f a corporation wants to enjoy the benefits of the privilege it should enforce a fairly firm 'need to know' [policy] of the communication rule.[19] In other words, forwarding e-mail messages to unnecessary recipients can destroy the confidentiality element needed to maintain the privilege.

Impact of Unsecured Technology on the Attorney-Client Privilege

When communications occur in circumstances where others can easily overhear, there is no expectation of confidentiality. The advent of technology that can be intercepted easily broadens the possibility of waiver of the privilege. For example, a cordless telephone is a two-way radio transmitter/receiver. Anyone within 1,000 feet who is listening with a scanner, compatible cordless telephone, or other radio receiver can intercept the conversation. Although it is a violation of federal and state law to intercept cellular telephone conversations, an Illinois court has held that persons using such phones do not have an expectation of confidentiality.[20]

Similarly, e-mail communications via the Internet may not enjoy the privacy protections one expects from an employer-operated e-mail system. Unlike private e-mail systems, the sender of an Internet e-mail message has no control over the routing, storage or access to the message either in transit or at the receiving address. Although very little case law exists on the subject, courts likely will refuse to find an expectation of privacy for e-mail sent over the Internet.

Advisory opinions issued by attorney bar groups in several states engage in a more detailed analysis of the issue. The prevailing approach of these opinions is that unencrypted e-mail to attorneys on routine matters carries with it the assurances of confidentiality, but highly sensitive matters require enhanced security. In an opinion released February 12, 1998, the District of Columbia Bar Legal Ethics Committee determined that except in extraordinary circumstances, unencrypted e-mail is an acceptable form of conveying client confidences, even where the lawyer does not obtain prior consent from the client. In addition, a 1998 law in New York state was added to the Civil Practice Law and Rules to ensure no attorney-client communication would lose its privileged status solely by virtue of being communicated by electronic means.

Keep in mind these same general principles that are considerations for dealings with outside counsel are equally applicable to communications that flow through the in-house school district legal department.

Precautions

As a precaution to prevent the inadvertent waiver of attorney-client privileged information, school districts should inform administrators about the rules surrounding the expectation of confidentiality. Armed with legal rules, administrators will be better able to take the practical precautions necessary when communicating with counsel. School districts also may wish to consider the use of encryption technology. Encryption is a method of scrambling electronic mail messages at their source, so that anyone who intercepts messages will be unable to read them. The intended recipient of the messages will have corresponding decryption software that renders the messages readable. Commercial and shareware encryption software are readily available. Encryption software can be purchased for a moderate price or can be obtained at certain Web sites for no cost whatsoever (see, for example, PGP Security, where a school district and its partner can both download a matching file encryption program for free—www.PGP.com/products/freeware/default.asp).

School Board Use of E-mail as a Public Meeting: State Sunshine Laws

With the rapid advancement in the technology of electronic communications has come the need for state legislatures to revise their Open Meetings Laws. These laws (commonly referred to as Sunshine Laws) generally require that meetings of school boards and other public bodies be conducted openly, so all interested persons are permitted to attend and listen to deliberations and proceedings. The policy behind these laws is the assurance that the public has access to information concerning the way the government conducts the public's business. But laws differ from one state to another.

The increased use of e-mail, virtual conferencing and other forms of interactive communications has created uncertainty in government agencies, including school boards, about whether such communications violate Sunshine Laws. When one board member sends an e-mail to other members about school board business, does that violate the state's Sunshine Law? What if members are using a simultaneous interaction (such as live chats) rather than a serial one? How about when board members use e-mail, telephones, or faxes to poll one another about board issues? While one might think these instances would be analogous to the use of telephones by board members, the issues are often more complicated.

Elected officials, therefore, should be cognizant of the requirements of their state's open meetings law and adhere carefully to its dictates. When in doubt, board members should avoid sending e-mails to everyone to poll fellow colleagues about public issues. A single e-mail copied to fellow board members or separate e-mails to each board member on a single public topic are roughly equivalent—and both could violate open meetings laws. For the same reason, board members should be cautious in using live, interactive technology to have a simultaneous electronic interchange of opinions.

Beware, also, that live, interactive technology is now generally available. Referred to as "groupware," it creates the equivalent of a limited access "chat room." Touted by advertisers as able to improve the efficiency of meetings and the flow of information in organizations, it allows long distance meetings at very low cost.

Lotus Development Corp. produces Lotus Notes® and Domino® as groupware products with a large market niche in both public schools and the corporate arena. Microsoft's Exchange® and Novell's Groupwise® are strong challengers. As more organizations create intranets, networks of significant data and collaborative capability are increasingly available.

Any business communication among a majority of board members transmitted via a chat room, groupware, intranet, electronic mailing list, or similar media is likely to be viewed by a court as a meeting subject to open meeting requirements.

No case involving the use of e-mail as a public meeting has reached the courts, but state legislatures and state attorneys general are pursuing clarification of the issue. A 1995 Kansas Attorney General's opinion found school board members may be in violation of the state Sunshine Law if a quorum of "board members *simultaneously* engage[s] in discussion of the board business through computer terminals."[21] The Kansas Sunshine Law defines "meeting" to include any "gathering, assembly, telephone call or any other means of *interactive communication*."[22] The attorney general opined that if "a sender of a message does not get an immediate response from a receiver, the communication is not *interactive*." Simply sending a message to other board members would not constitute an "interactive communication" as defined by law.[23]

What Is a "Meeting"?
Excerpts from State Sunshine Laws

California... amended its Sunshine Law, the Brown Act, in 1994 to define "meeting" as "...any use of direct communication, personal intermediaries, or technological devices that is employed by a majority of the members..." (Cal. Govt. Code Ann. 654952.2, West, 1998).

Montana... characterizes "meeting" as "the convening of a quorum ... whether corporal or by means of electronic equipment to hear, discuss or act upon a matter...." (Mont. Code Ann. 62-3-202, West, 1997).

Colorado... defines "meeting" as "any kind of gathering convened to discuss public business, in person, by telephone, electronically, or by other means of communication. (Col. Rev. Stat. Ann. 624-6-402, West, 1998).

Virginia... provides in its state Freedom of Information Act that any governing body conducting a meeting where the "public business is discussed or transacted through telephonic video, electronic or other communication means where the members are not physically present" violates the law. (1950 Va. Code Ann. 62.1-343.1., Michie, 1998).

A 1998 Kansas Attorney General's opinion on open meetings went further, declaring that a series of meetings, each of which involves less than a majority of a quorum, but collectively totaling a majority of a quorum, at which there is a common topic of discussion of the business or affairs of that body constitutes a meeting for purposes of the Kansas Open Meetings Act.[24] An example would be a communication tree in which the chair e-mails board members one by one and asks their opinion on a controversial topic. In that case, no more than two board members would be "speaking" to each other at a time, but the survey would violate Kansas law because it is, in effect, "conducting business," only not in public. Similarly, the Attorney General said, if one board member e-mails another, who adds to the e-mail and sends it along to the next, that would violate the law. The same would be true of a group mailing list in which each member automatically receives messages posted by others, and can comment on the messages. Each would be circumventing the law, according to the opinion, because members could exchange their thoughts on a public issue without ever gathering or communicating in real time under public scrutiny.

Compare the Kansas opinion, however, to *Del Papa v. Board of Regents of the University and Community College System of Nevada*.[25] In *Del Papa*, the Nevada Supreme Court held, "a quorum of a public body using *serial communication* to deliberate toward a decision ... on any matter over which the public body has supervision" violates the state's Sunshine Law.[26] In that case, the chairman of the Board of Regents sent faxes to board members requesting their opinions about whether to issue a media statement condemning public criticism of board activities by one of its members. All board members received faxes except the member who had made the public criticisms. The board members responded to the chairman's inquiry by telephone, and the chairman ultimately decided not to issue the media statement.

In finding the Board violated the state Sunshine Law by using telephones and faxes to transact Board of Regents business, the court based its analysis on the

Four Ways for School Boards to Reconcile Open Meeting Laws and the Use of Electronic Communication

1. School board members must be well-informed as to their legal responsibilities when using electronic communications. They must understand their state's Open Meeting Laws and appreciate when an e-mail or fax may trigger those laws.

2. E-mails and faxes to other board members by themselves generally do not implicate Open Meeting Laws. The mere exchange of ideas and information between two board members is not the conduct of public business. It is not the deliberative process that Sunshine Laws demand be open to public scrutiny.

3. Simultaneous or serial communications generally will implicate Open Meeting Laws. These communications begin to form the give-and-take that characterizes the deliberative process and should be done in an open forum. Public business usually includes the adoption of any proposed policy, resolution, rule or other formal action, and any deliberative activities on those matters.

4. E-meetings often can allow absent board members to participate in important public issues, thereby supporting the representative nature of board work. Generally, however, there should be a quorum present at a physical location where the press and public are present, and the press and public should have the same access to the electronic input as the board members. This can be accomplished by speaker phones for telephone meetings, or with projectors or large screens for computer-based information or communication.

Maine School Boards Association E-mail Use Policy
School Board Use of Electronic Mail

Use of electronic mail (e-mail) by school board members should conform to the same standards of judgement, propriety and ethics as other forms of school board-related communication. Board members shall comply with the following guidelines when using e-mail in the conduct of board responsibilities:

A. The School Board shall not use e-mail as a substitute for deliberations at Board meetings or for other communications or business properly confined to Board meetings.

B. Board members should be aware that e-mail and e-mail attachments received or prepared for use in board business or containing information relating to board business are likely to be regarded as public records which may be inspected by any person upon request, unless otherwise made confidential by law.

C. Board members should avoid reference to confidential information about employees, students or other matters in e-mail communications because of the risk of improper disclosure. Board members should comply with the same standards as school employees with regard to confidential information.

[NOTE: Local school units, which provide e-mail/Internet access to Board members, may want to include additional guidelines concerning the use of passwords.]

Source: National Education Policy Network (Code: BEA), National School Boards Association, June 2000.

definition of "meeting." The court also relied on case law in other jurisdictions, holding that the making of decisions by public bodies using either telephone or mail polls without public attendance constitutes a meeting and therefore violates the spirit of the state's Sunshine Law. Finally, the court relied on a provision in the state code declaring that "electronic communication ... must not be used to circumvent the spirit or letter of the [Sunshine Law]."[27]

A 1998 Florida Attorney General opinion concluded that because state law required school boards to meet at "a public place in the county," a quorum of the school board must be physically present. The board, however, could use electronic means to enable a minority of members who were absent to be included.

In Wisconsin, a 1996 Attorney General opinion indicated that an e-mail poll of board members to determine whether they would enter into a contract was a violation of that state's Open Meeting law.

The varying conclusions in these decisions illustrate the disparity among state laws in this area. A survey of state Sunshine Laws suggests some states still operate under old Sunshine Laws and make no mention of electronic communications while others have amended their statutes to include such provisions.

To determine whether board members have complied with a state's Sunshine Law, courts will also review the substance of the communication that occurred. Once again, the determination depends on the language of the statute at issue, but most statutes prohibit private communications among board members only where "public business" is being transacted. Public business usually includes the adoption of any proposed policy, resolution, rule, or other formal action.[28] It might also include deliberations on those same matters. These varying statutes demonstrate the need for public officials to be well informed about the laws in their state.

Many state Sunshine Laws and "Public Records Acts" require public access to certain records. Again, statutes vary widely, but most require that records documenting policies, decisions, procedures, and other operations of public offices be made available to the public. The issue for schools and other public agencies is whether e-mail communications between board members constitute public records for purposes of state law.[29] This inquiry raises many difficult questions. Should all e-mail communications be archived as is required of other documents? How well are public agents equipped to act as official custodians of such communications and to determine whether or not they are public records?

Best Practices in Board Member Use of Technology

- Develop an acceptable use policy applicable to all users, including school board members, that is reasonable and enforceable. Then, enforce it consistently.

- Treat all electronic communications as potentially subject to the Freedom of Information Act (FOIA).

- Board members would be well advised to keep public and personal communication totally separate. Do not put personal messages in e-mails discussing public business.

- Archive all e-mail discussing school business in the same manner as you archive physical documents. Store backup discs or drives for the statutorily prescribed time period.

When responding to FOIA requests, if in doubt consider two factors: 1) the source of the message and, 2) the content of the message. If the source is a personal computer and the content does not relate to school business, the message is protected as not being a public record. If the e-mail is sent or received on a school computer and relates to school business, clearly it is subject to disclosure.

The Colorado Legislature attempted to address these issues in its Sunshine Law.[30] That statute specifies only e-mail used "to discuss pending legislation or other public business" shall be subject to the Sunshine Law, and state law does not cover e-mail communications about any other topics.[31] While such legislation may give some guidance to state agents in determining whether communications are covered by law, the language is still vague and open to interpretation by courts.

In passing legislation to clarify the use of e-mail as public records, legislatures must engage in balancing the policy of providing wide access to government information and activities against the privacy interests and practical limitations of public officials and employees.[32] E-mail is a useful tool for state officials to gather information and communicate with staff, other officials, agencies, and the public. Legislatures are challenged with trying to protect such communications while also protecting public access to public information.

In *Tiberino v. Spokane County Wash.*,[33] the court ruled that e-mail messages that are sent and received by county employees are public records under Washington state law but are not subject to disclosure because they constitute personal information. The ruling explained that while the number of personal messages sent or received by a person who is paid to perform government duties is a matter of public concern, the contents are personal in nature and outside the realm of interests promoted by the state open records law.

These materials demonstrate that as technological communications continue to advance, school board members will have to adjust their behavior. In some jurisdictions, individual e-mail communication among board members may not violate state law while in others it may be a clear violation. Other forms of interactive communication (such as virtual conferencing, chat rooms, and instant messaging systems) accentuate the need for school board members to recognize the implications of all forms of board communication. Members should be familiar with state laws governing such communications, and where uncertainty exists they should seek the advice of counsel. Since most statutes provide for the nullification of board decisions that violate state Sunshine Laws, school board members would be well advised to take preemptive action to determine what types of communication are implicated by law.

For a discussion of e-mail, student records, and the Family Educational Rights and Privacy Act (FERPA) see Chapter 1. For a general discussion of e-mail records and employees, see Chapter 3.

ADA Compliance for Web Sites

The Americans with Disabilities Act (ADA)

According to the most recent statistics, more than 54 million people in the United States—about one in every five people—have a disability.[34] In 1997, 8 percent of children ages 5 to 17, or about 4 million school-aged children, were limited in their activities because of one or more chronic health conditions.[35]

To protect those with disabilities, Congress passed the Americans with Disabilities Act (ADA) in 1990. The ADA prohibits discrimination on the basis of disability in employment, programs and services provided by state and local governments, goods and services provided by private companies, and in commercial facilities. The ADA also requires state and local governments to provide access to programs offered to the public. It covers effective communication with people who have disabilities and requires reasonable modifications of policies and practices that may tend to discriminate against the disabled. [For more on this topic, see *Technology for Students with Disabilities: A Decision Maker's Resource Guide*, published in 1998 by the National School Boards Association and the U.S. Department of Education's Office of Special Education Programs.]

School Compliance

As government entities providing programs and services, public schools are covered by the Americans with Disabilities Act and must comply with its provisions.[36] Schools must provide reasonable accommodation to individuals with disabilities unless doing so would result in a fundamental alteration to the program or service or create an undue burden on the school. Compliance includes ensuring access not only to public educational facilities but also to communications. Whenever schools communicate information regarding their programs, goods, or services, they must provide appropriate auxiliary aids or services to ensure effective communication with individuals who have disabilities. Such communications include print and audio media, as well as computerized media such as Web sites found on the Internet.

Thousands of schools in the United States and across the world have developed Web sites to provide information to the public and experience for the students who create and maintain the sites. Sites include information about and links to academic programs, faculty, student organizations, parent-teacher associations, school board policies, Internet-use policies, school newspapers, and even school lunches. They are important resources for schools, and their use is rapidly increasing. Unfortunately, many schools are only beginning to realize the need to make their Web sites accessible to individuals with disabilities. Students and others with disabilities who are denied effective access to school Web pages may have a cause of action against the school under the ADA and parallel state statutes. Schools can preempt such action by being proactive in establishing universal access to all sources of communication, including Web sites.

What Is the Problem?

The problem for schools and other institutions is that Web sites that are perfectly accessible to most people may be impossible to access for students with disabilities. With the advancement of technology, the World Wide Web has gone from using a simple text-based format to using a robust design format that includes widely used graphics, tables, photographs, and video and audio clips.

Individuals with vision impairments must rely on screen readers or voice command software to read text aloud from Web pages, but such tools cannot read graphics or video clips. For a blind person, Web sites that rely on graphics can slow navigation to a crawl, and where the graphic provides vital information or is used to move around the screen (such as an arrow button), it may make navigation altogether impossible. People with hearing disabilities are also at a disadvantage because they cannot access audio clips unless they are provided access to a text version. Because schools must provide communication to those with disabilities that is *as effective as that provided to others*,[37] schools must use universal design principles to make their sites widely accessible. *Universal design* is the development of information systems that are flexible enough to accommodate the needs and preferences of the broadest range of users of computers and telecommunications equipment, regardless of age or disability.

How to Comply

Fortunately, making a Web site universally accessible is not as difficult as it sounds. By using the following Disability Access Design Standards developed by the city of San Jose, California,[38] schools should be able to make their sites universally accessible and comply with the ADA at the same time:

1) *Assess Your Web Site.* First, view your current Web site to see how accessible it is. Start by using a text-based Internet browser that has no capability for graphics or fancy fonts. This browser will enable you to move around your home page and

determine whether or not all your links are visible. If you select a link and the page reads only [image] [image] [image], you know you have a problem. The link is relying on graphics, and a blind visitor using voice command software will not be able to see (or rather hear) what the image is. Instead, the visitor will hear only the word "image" instead of a description of the image. Determine whether the page still makes sense without the graphics, tables, or columns or whether providing a textual description would suffice as an alternative. Assess each trouble spot, and use the following measures to address them.

2) *Provide an Access Instruction Page.* This page should provide instructions for access to your Web site for users with disabilities. It should be linked to your home page and ideally should provide an e-mail hyperlink for visitors to communicate problems they have with Web page accessibility.

3) *Supply Support for Text Browsers.* Access to support should be available directly on the page itself or should be provided by an alternative text page displaying the same information.

4) *Provide Alternatives to PDFs.* Documents posted in Portable Document Format (PDF) cannot be read by most screen readers, so a second version should be posted in an accessible format utilizing ASCII or text HTML.

5) *Use "Alt" Tags.* Attach an "Alt" tag to each graphic image, and provide a short description of that image.

6) *Hyperlink Photographs with "D."* Link photographs on the page with a description button ("D") which can be used as a selectable hyperlink to a description of the photograph. Use a "Return" hyperlink at the end of the description to return the user to the photograph.

7) *Hyperlink Audio and Video Clips with "CC."* Link audio and video clips with a closed-caption ("CC") link button that provides text transcriptions or descriptions.

8) *Use Descriptive Words as Links.* Avoid using words such as "click here" that do not convey information about the nature of the link.

9) *Provide Alternative Mechanisms for Access to Online Forms and for Downloading Software.* Since all browsers do not support all online forms (such as application forms), and screen readers may not be able to download software, provide phone numbers or e-mail addresses for users to access forms or assistance.

10) *Avoid Using Formats That Create Barriers.* Formats such as frames, tables, and newspaper formats are not accessible by all browsers or screen readers and should be avoided wherever possible. Where they are necessary to the integrity of the page, provide proper descriptions of each.

The United States government has also mandated accessibility standards for electronic and information technology under Section 508 of the Rehabilitation Act, as amended.[39] On December 21, 2000, the Access Board, an independent agency specializing in access issues for people with disabilities, issued its final guidelines, which became effective on June 21, 2001.

The law applies to all types of electronic and information technology in the federal sector, including all government Web sites. It applies to existing electronics as well as to those that will be purchased after the effective date. It directs that federal agencies make technology accessible to employees and the public to the extent it does not pose an "undue burden." Many of the mandates reflect the San Jose standards listed above.

While the federal law does not apply to local units like schools, it may contain some ideas for districts and some useful examples of sound practice.

Affirmative Duty

Courts have held that public entities have an "affirmative duty" under the ADA to evaluate their policies and procedures addressing services and programs for individuals with disabilities.[40] This affirmative duty means it is not enough to respond on an ad hoc basis to complaints or requests for accommodations, but rather policies must be formulated in advance, and the community of persons with disabilities must be consulted in the development of the policies.[41] A proactive approach is what is expected and anticipated by the law. This means schools implementing new Web sites must ensure they are accessible from the beginning, and those with Web sites not yet in compliance must correct the problem as soon as possible. Furthermore, schools must not merely provide access to students and other individuals with disabilities but also ensure the communication is equally effective.

Ensuring Accessibility

While public policy and the ADA require the removal of barriers to effective communication, such compliance has other benefits as well. Ensuring universal design of Web sites makes the sites highly usable and available to everyone. For instance, many users lack state-of-the-art technologies to access high-tech Web sites. Broad access is important because many visitors to the Web don't have the most updated browser software and cannot otherwise access a school's Web page. Additionally, many users get online access through devices such as Palm Pilots or WebTV, or even through their telephones. Making changes to accommodate people with disabilities ensures access for everyone. It gives high-tech users the tools and graphics necessary to keep the site fun and interesting while allowing the low-tech or disabled user equally effective access and communication.

Physical Security of Technological Equipment

Security has become a major concern as technology becomes more prevalent in schools. While the legal rules surrounding theft or damage to high-tech equipment are the same as for all other school property, administrators must take special precautions to protect their investment in such equipment. Policies must be instituted and followed to prevent theft, vandalism, and misuse of equipment in both school- and district-level operations.

Equipment such as laptop computers and software is easily transportable and should be secured when not in use. To facilitate repair, newer computers are designed for easy removal of components (such as hard drives) that therefore are easily stolen unless properly secured. Computers themselves can have lock-down capabilities that should be utilized, and security systems can be used so an alarm will sound if wires are cut. Network hubs and other equipment to which few people need access should be kept in separate, lockable facilities. Areas not open to the public will require less attention than those widely accessible. Like all other aspects of the implementation of a technology plan, schools should assess their current and future security needs prior to the installation of computers and other electronic equipment.

Internet Access and the E-rate

Access to the Internet is one of the most important aspects of a technology system. While computers and software provide valuable tools for learning, it is the Internet that opens the door to the unlimited world of online information. But as with other technologies, schools must pay for access to the Internet. Now the federal government has enacted legislation to help schools in that endeavor.

In 1996, Congress passed the Telecommunications Act,[42] one of its broadest funding mechanisms ever. The purpose was to ensure that all Americans, particularly those living in low-income, rural, and high-cost service areas, have access to affordable, quality telecommunications services.

The Telecommunications Act established the Universal Service Fund, commonly called the E-rate. The E-rate was created to provide the nation's elementary and secondary schools and libraries with deep discounts (20 to 90 percent) for services such as basic telephone service, advanced telecommunications services, Internet services, and internal connections. The program is financed by a surcharge placed on monthly telephone bills, so the money comes from telephone companies rather than from taxes. The amount of the discount awarded each school is tied to the school's location (rural or urban) and economic need as determined by the level of eligibility for federal free and reduced-price school lunch programs. The Schools and Libraries Corporation (now the Schools and Libraries Division of the Universal Service Administrative Company) was created to administer and manage the application and funding process.

As part of the application process, schools applying for the discounts must submit a budget and a technology plan that meets certain criteria. The plan must include the school's strategy for providing professional development and for purchasing necessary hardware and software. Approval of plans may be granted by certain state education agencies. Additionally, schools must conduct a technology inventory and assessment of the telecommunications services it already uses, as well as those it intends to purchase. In order to qualify for funding, schools must certify that they have Internet blocking or filtering software to prevent children from having access to sexually explicit, or other, unacceptable material. This requirement is part of the Children's Internet Protection Act and applies to the E-rate funding cycle that begins July 1, 2001 and all subsequent funding cycles.

While the discounts available will be helpful to schools in obtaining telecommunications services, the E-rate does not provide for the cost of items such as hardware and software. In addition, the application procedure has been criticized by some as complex and cumbersome. Nevertheless, funds are available annually and eligible schools should take advantage of the E-rate to complement the many tools necessary to implement a technology system.

Yet, as of Summer 2001, the Federal Communications Commission (FCC) was pondering how to resolve a dilemma—that E-rate requests are now far outstripping the resources available to accommodate them. The FCC is considering a rule that would give funding priority to schools that did not receive funds for internal wiring in 2000.

The E-rate has been an effective initiative to equip the nation's schools and libraries with telecommunications technology. According to a May 2001 report by the National Center for Education Statistics (http://www.nces.ed.gov), about 98 percent of public schools are now connected to the Internet.

R. Craig Wood is a partner and litigation department head in the Charlottesville, Virginia office of McGuireWoods LLP. He practices education law, labor and employment law and commercial litigation, and teaches trial advocacy at the University of Virginia School of Law. Special thanks is given to Patrick J. Dolan, a student at the University of Virginia School of Law, for his assistance in updating this chapter.

This chapter revises and updates "Administrative Issues in School Technology," by Rodney A. Satterwhite, Calvin S. Spencer, Jr., and R. Craig Wood. Legal Issues & Education Technology: A School Leader's Guide (1999), Alexandria, VA: National School Boards Association.

Resources

Electronic Resources

Bobby - a Web site that will perform a free accessibility diagnostic and suggest corrective action and improvements
http://www.cast.org/bobby

City of San Jose. 1998, August. *World Wide Web Page Disability Access Design Standards.*
http://www.ci.san-jose.ca.us/oaacc/disacces.html

Education and Library Networks Coalition (EdLinc) - Coalition members consists of national organizations representing public schools (including NSBA), private schools, libraries, and rural community groups. It seeks to expand the availability of education technologies and has worked to secure enactment and full implementation of the E-Rate telecommunications discounts for schools and libraries.
http://www.edlinc.org

LearnNet - the informal education Web page of the Federal Communications Commission (FCC)
http://www.fcc.gov/learnnet

National Research Council. 1997. *More Than Screen Deep: Toward Every-Citizen Interfaces to the Nation's Information Infrastructure.* Washington, DC: National Academy Press.
http://nap.edu/catalog/5780.html

Schools and Libraries Division (SLD) - an independent not-for-profit corporation established under the 1996 Telecommunications Act to administer universal service programs for schools & libraries. SLD administers the E-Rate program.
http://www.sl.universalservice.org

U.S. Access Board - an independent federal agency devoted to accessibility for people with disabilities
http://www.access-board.gov

U.S. Department of Education's Office of Educational Technology (OET) - develops national education technology policy and implements this policy through department-wide education technology programs. The site includes recent legislative and budget updates, grant announcements, and links to department and other federal technology-related publications.
http://www.ed.gov/Technology

Waddell, Cynthia D. 1998, June 17. Paper presented at the National Conference of the American Bar Association. *Applying the ADA to the Internet: A Web Accessibility Standard.*
http://www.rit.edu/~easi/law/weblaw1.htm

Web Accessibility Resources. 2001. Disabilities & Computing Program, University of California, Los Angeles.
http://www.dcp.ucla.edu/

World Wide Web Consortium (W3C) Web Accessibility Initiative - W3C engages in a number of national and international activities designed to maximize the Web's potential. The Web Accessibility Initiative (WAI), in coordination with organizations around the world, pursues accessibility of the Web through five primary areas of work: technology, guidelines, tools, education and outreach, and research and development. It is currently developing Web Content Accessibility Guidelines 2.0, as well other guidelines that enhance Web usability for people with disabilities. http://w3.org/WAI

Print Resources

Technology for students with disabilities: A decision maker's resource guide. 1997. Alexandria, VA: National School Boards Association and the U.S. Department of Education, Office of Special Education and Rehabilitative Services.

Waddell, Cynthia D., and Kevin Lee Thomason. 1998, November. **Is your site ADA-compliant?** *The Internet Lawyer* 4(11).

Endnotes

1 "Futurework: Trends and Challenges for Work in the 21st Century," Occupational Outlook Quarterly, U.S. Department of Labor, Summer 2000, Volume 44, Number 2.

2 *See Harris v. Forklift Systems, Inc.*, 114 S.Ct. 367 (1993).

3 928 F. Supp. 533 (E.D. Pa. 1996)

4 904 F.2d 853 (3d Cir. N.J. 1990)

5 Several states, including Minnesota and California, have enacted legislation prohibiting sexual harassment in schools.

6 *See Burlington Industries, Inc. v. Ellerth*, 118 S. Ct. 2257, 2270 (1998).

7 *Id.*

8 *See Franklin v. Gwinett County Pub. Sch.*, 503 U.S. 60, 63 (1992).

9 524 U.S. 274 (1998)

10 526 U.S. 629 (1999)

11 *E.g., Wilson-Simmons v. Lake County Sheriff's Dept.*, 982 F. Supp. 496 (N.D. Ohio 1997); *Keppler v. GPU, Inc.*, 2 F. Supp. 2d 730 (W.D. Pa. 1998); *Strauss v. Microsoft Corp.*, 856 F. Supp. 821 (S.D.N.Y. 1994).

12 93 F.3d 1327 (7th Cir. 1996)

13 *See also Vicarelli v. Business Int.'l Inc.*, 973 F. Supp. 241 (D.Mass. 1997).

14 The Federal Rules of Civil Procedure provide that documents include "writings, drawings, graphs, charts, photographs, phone records and other data compilations from which information can be obtained, translated, if necessary, by the respondent through detection devices into reasonably useable form. . ." Fed. R. Civ. P. 34(a).

15 *See In re Brand Name Prescription Drugs Antitrust Litigation*, 1995 U.S. Dist. LEXIS 18048 (N.D.Ill. 1995) (unpublished disposition).

16 *See Proctor & Gamble v. Haugen*, 179 F.R.D. 622 (D.Utah 1998).

17   *Id.*

18   150 F.R.D. 465, 491 (S.D.N.Y. 1993)

19   *See also Jonathan Corp. v. Prime Computer, Inc.*, 114 F.R.D. 693, 696 (E.D. Va. 1987) ("It should be noted, however, that by virtue of Prime's failure to indicate on the face of the memorandum that the document was confidential or contained attorney-client privileged information, coupled with the fact that the memorandum was distributed to six (6) employees, this court has serious doubts as to whether [the party] has met its burden of demonstrating that the document was intended to be confidential.")

20   *People v. Wilson*, 196 Ill.App.3d 997, 1010 (1990) appeal denied, 133 Ill.2d 571 (1990); *See also Illinois Attorney General's Opinion*, 1994 Ill. AG LEXIS 10.

21   Kan. Atty. Gen. Op. No. 95-13, 1995 WL 40761 (Kan. A.G.) (Emphasis added). Open Meetings Law: K.S.A. 75-4317a.

22   *Id.*

23   *Id.*

24   Kan. Atty. Gen. Op. No. 98-26 (April 20, 1998).

25   956 P.2d 770 (Nev., 1998).

26   *Id.* at 778.

27   *Id.* at 773.

28   See Col. Rev. Stat. Ann. §24-6-402.2(c) (West, 1998).

29   See *generally, State v. Lake County Sheriff's Department*, 693 N.E.2d 789 (Ohio, 1998).

30   Col. Rev. Stat. Ann. §24-6-402.2(d)(III). (West, 1998).

31   *Id.*

32   Col. Rev. Stat. Ann. §24-6-402 (West, 1998).

33   Wash. Ct. App., 3d Div., No. 18830-2-III (December 14, 2000)

34   *Study: Disabled Workers Left Out of Prosperity*, The Times Union, November 4, 2000; *Work and the Disabled*, N.Y. Times, January 8, 2001.

35   1997 National Health Interview Survey, National Center for Health Statistics, U.S. Center for Disease Control.

36   The Supreme Court has determined that the Eleventh Amendment to the Constitution bars damage actions against states and state agencies under the ADA, but compliance and injunctive remedies are still available. *Board of Trustees v. Garrett*, 2001 U.S. LEXIS 1700 (U.S. Feb. 21, 2001).

37   U.S. Dept. of Education, Office of Civil Rights, Settlement Letter: Docket #09-95-2205 (1996 Letter).

38   City of San Jose, *World Wide Web Page, Disability Access Design Standards* (http://www.ci.san-jose.ca.us/oaacc/disaccess.html).

39   *See* Access Board, www.access-board.gov

40   *Tyler v. City of Manhattan*, 857 F. Supp. 800 (D.Kans. 1994).

41   *Id.*

42   47 USCS §609 et seq.

Chapter 3

Legal Considerations in Regulating Employee Use of School Technology

Bruce W. Smith, Esq.
Drummond Woodsum & MacMahon
Portland, ME

Introduction

Schools have invested vast sums of money in the acquisition and networking of Internet-connected computers for educators. This investment is justified by the educational value that computer technology provides. It should come as no surprise, however, that school employees are apparently no less likely than employees in other workplaces to misuse or abuse computer technology; such misuse ranges from the merely unproductive to the illegal. With the widespread use of computer technology comes the need for school leaders to regulate such use with due regard for both applicable legal constraints and the practical realities of employee access to computers.

Regulation of computer use in the public school setting poses special challenges because public employees are involved. This chapter addresses several issues relating to staff access to computers: personal use and privacy issues; collective bargaining; First Amendment concerns; rules governing staff computer use; and employee safety. The primary theme of the chapter is that by anticipating and understanding these issues, schools will best be able to manage the challenges they present.

Personal Use of School District Computers

Despite falling prices, a personal computer is an extremely expensive piece of equipment, generally far more expensive than any other single tool provided by schools to their teachers. Most schools have determined, though, that the educational benefit justifies the investment. Research has repeatedly shown that technology in the classroom can improve the creativity, research skills, and higher-level thinking skills of students.[1] Empirical data have also shown that, in some settings, students who effectively use computer systems outperform those who don't by 25 percent to 41 percent.[2] These data, coupled with other measures and teacher observations, demonstrate that technology can have a positive impact in the classroom.

Having endorsed significant spending on technology for students, teachers, and other staff members, school districts should also take reasonable measures to protect that investment and to prevent educationally counter-productive uses of the technology.

The temptation for staff members to make personal use of school computers, particularly those connected to the Internet and/or schoolwide networks, is probably

> *"School districts have substantial discretion to prevent or regulate personal use of their computers. If they fail to exercise that discretion in a deliberate manner, however, they may find the district's computers, by default, become used in an unfettered fashion by staff members for inappropriate personal use."*

irresistible. In certain cases, personal use is approved as a means for teachers to become more knowledgeable about computer technology. School districts sometimes encourage employees to use district-owned technology as a means of familiarizing themselves with the function and range of features available for educational applications.

On the other hand, excessive personal use can interfere with the performance of job duties. The content of some employee e-mail communications is sometimes inappropriate or even harmful in the school environment. School employees have on occasion used the Internet to view or download materials that are clearly inappropriate in any public school.

Another twist is that a school district that stores the e-mails of employees may be asked to disclose them to the media or other private party via a freedom of information request. That was the scenario in *Tiberino v. Spokane County*,[3]. The case involved a secretary, employed by the county, who was dismissed based on her unsatisfactory work performance and personal use of e-mails. A newspaper and television station then requested a copy of the e-mails. The court concluded that while the e-mails are public records, and even the volume of e-mail can be disclosed, the content of the e-mails is personal and therefore outside the scope of a public records request.

The Washington state act conditioned disclosure of a record on the fact that it contained "information relating to the conduct of government or the performance of any governmental or proprietary function." The court held that the public has an interest in seeing that public employees are not spending their time on the public payroll pursuing personal interests. "But it is the amount of time spent on personal matters, not the content of personal e-mails or phone calls or conversations, that is of public interest," the opinion proclaimed. The court added, "The fact that Ms. Tiberino sent 467 e-mails over a 40 working-day time frame is of significance in her termination action… [B]ut what she said in those e-mails is of no public significance."

School districts have substantial discretion to prevent or regulate personal use of their computers. If they fail to exercise that discretion in a deliberate manner, however, they may find the district's computers, by default, become used in an unfettered fashion by staff members for inappropriate personal use. Once that occurs, there may be legal and political hurdles that make it more difficult to reassert control over the district's computer systems. *See "Rules & Policies for Employee Use of School Computers" later in this chapter for ideas on how to regulate employee use.*

Privacy

One of the more common questions concerning employee use of school computers is this: To what extent, if any, is information stored on, sent from, or received by employee computers private? Often employees assume that their computers, even though supplied by the school, are part of a private zone to which supervisors and other employees do not have access. But their subjective belief that such material is private will not necessarily prevent school administrators from having access to it if the right policies have been adequately distributed and evenly enforced.

The common strand underlying the various legal theories concerning employee computer privacy is that the employee must have a "**reasonable** expectation of privacy" in the material if the employee is going to assert a successful legal challenge. The employees' **reasonable** expectations regarding privacy, or the lack of it, are largely determined by the employer's policies, rules, and practices concerning use of the school computer system. By developing and distributing those rules, the school is able to define the zone of privacy, if any, that staff members have. Additionally, even where an employee has a reasonable expectation of privacy, the U.S. Supreme Court has ruled that an employer will not be found to have violated the employee's privacy right if the employer acted reasonably under the circumstances.[4]

"In order to retain the maximum degree of legal authority to search computer files and networks, however, schools should consider establishing very clear rules stating that school officials can and will search data or e-mail stored on all school-owned computers at any time for any reason, and that staff members have no right of privacy in any such data."

So, should employee acceptable use policies (AUPs) or rules give staff members any privacy interests in e-mail or stored files? As a practical matter, school administrators probably have no desire to review all e-mail or to scour computer hard drives on a regular basis. In order to retain the maximum degree of legal authority to search computer files and networks, however, schools should consider establishing very clear rules stating that school officials can and will search data or e-mail stored on all school-owned computers at any time for any reason, and that staff members have no right of privacy in any such data. Such rules will come in handy in a variety of legal circumstances.

Experience demonstrates that there are good reasons for retaining the right to access employees' computers. This writer has dealt with numerous cases involving misuse of school computer communications, including but not limited to: a teacher sending sexually explicit e-mails to a former student; one teacher sexually harassing another; a principal distributing off-color jokes to other employees; teachers sending abusive or rude e-mails to their supervisors; teachers communicating with students in an inappropriate manner; teachers accessing pornographic Web sites during school hours; and teachers "day trading" stocks during school hours. In order to investigate properly and prove such misuse, schools must have immediate access to staff computers. The likelihood of authorities checking could also act as a deterrent.

The practice of monitoring electronic communications at work is becoming more prevalent. A study released on July 9, 2001 by the Privacy Foundation (http://www.privacyfoundation.org/resources/14million.asp) concluded that more than one-third of U.S. employees who browse the Web and use e-mail on the job are monitored by their employers. The study attributed the growing popularity of the practice to inexpensive surveillance software, concerns about productivity, and liability for sexual harassment. Around the world, of the more than 100 million workers with Internet access, approximately 27 million of them are monitored.

Federal Law

As government employees, school staffs have a right under the Fourth Amendment of the U.S. Constitution to be free from unreasonable searches and seizures. The United States Supreme Court ruled in *O'Connor v. Ortega*[5] that the Fourth Amendment applies only when a public employee has "an expectation of privacy that society is prepared to consider reasonable." Whether such an expectation exists depends upon the circumstances, including the employer's policies and practices. That said, school boards can purposefully act to erase an expectation of privacy by passing a comprehensive policy—in essence putting employees on notice that personal privacy does not apply for school-owned computers. That becomes important because if the employee has a reasonable expectation of privacy, the public employer is restricted and may conduct a work search only if "reasonable under all the circumstances."

It is likely a court would apply this rule to searches of employee computer files and electronic mail. If the employee has a reasonable expectation of privacy in those files, the employer must have a reasonable basis to review them in order to comply with the Fourth Amendment.

The Federal Electronic Communications Privacy Act[6] (ECPA) also protects the privacy of electronic communications, including electronic mail. The 1986 act contains an exception for the provider of the electronic communications service, which generally is viewed as including employers who provide a computer system or portable laptop for use by employees at work or on work-related tasks.[7] In addition, the ECPA does not apply when an individual has consented to the monitoring.

The Federal Wiretap Act[8] *et seq.* is yet another way under ECPA that an employee might seek to prevent school districts from seeing the contents of an e-mail communication. The act prohibits the "interception" of private communications. In *Fraser v. Nationwide Mutual Insurance Co.*[9] the court ruled that the Federal Wiretap Act does not apply after the communication has already been transmitted and when an employer acquires the electronic mail from a post-transmission storage file. In this case, a Nationwide agent leased a computer from the company, and each time he logged on there appeared an information box that said "for everyone's mutual protection [the] system use, including electronic e-mail, may be monitored to protect against unauthorized use." A review of the agent's computer files led to the discovery that he had sent a letter to competitors encouraging them to solicit Nationwide policyholders. He challenged the practice and lost.

Generally speaking, then, the ECPA is not likely to present a significant obstacle to school district monitoring of employee e-mail communications. The best way to ensure the law is not violated, however, is to have in place a policy notifying employees that their e-mail is not private and that it will be monitored, and to disseminate that policy to all employees.

Another potential legal basis for a right to privacy in computer files and e-mail is the "common law" right to privacy.[10] An employee whose e-mail has been reviewed by the employer may file a common law suit in court for invasion of privacy. The tort of invasion of privacy requires the intrusion into privacy be "highly offensive to a reasonable person."[11] The employee must have a reasonable expectation of privacy in the material reviewed in order to prevail on such a claim.

In the few court decisions addressing whether employer interception of employee e-mail constitutes an invasion of privacy, courts have rejected the claims. For example:

- In an unpublished decision by the Court of Appeals of Texas,[12] the court addressed a claim by a Microsoft employee that the company's review of his personal e-mail was an invasion of privacy. The employee had computer folders designated "personal" in which he stored his personal e-mail; these personal folders were protected by the employee's self-created password. Microsoft had gained access to these folders. The employee argued that since Microsoft had allowed employees to keep personal e-mail folders with their own separate passwords, the company had recognized an employee's right to privacy. There was no mention in the case that Microsoft had any employee e-mail policy or that the employee had signed any form acknowledging the employer's right of access to e-mail. The Court ruled that the employee had no legitimate expectation of privacy in his personal folders because the computer was supplied by Microsoft so that he could do his job, and that the e-mails had been transmitted over the employer's network and were accessible by third parties. Thus the court rejected the employee's invasion of privacy claim.

- In a California Superior Court case, the employee had signed a waiver acknowledging that e-mail use was limited to "company business," and thus could not complain about employer access to the e-mail.[13]

- In a Pennsylvania case, the employee had sent the e-mail to his supervisor, so he could not claim that he had a reasonable expectation of privacy.[14]

Computer Data as Evidence

Computers are designed to retain data of all kinds, resulting in the preservation of a great deal of information that simply would not have been available in the past. Documents that would once have been discarded now often end up saved unintentionally in computer files on individual hard drives or on network servers. Communications that would once have occurred orally by telephone or face-to-face are now memorialized in electronic mail. Research that might have left no tangible record in the past is now available for the asking because the session is preserved in Web browser logs. The availability of all this information may prove to be a useful tool to schools when allegations of employee misconduct are investigated.

Thus, not only does technology provide new means for employee misconduct, it also provides a new means for gathering evidence about misconduct. Indeed, in many cases that do not involve these technologies directly, evidence of the misconduct may be found in an e-mail or on an employee's hard drive or Web site. For example, while a teacher may not have used the e-mail system to harass another employee, there may be notes, a schedule, or other information stored in the teacher's computer that may confirm or refute the allegations. As with misconduct that involves direct misuse of these technologies, the school needs to access the employee's computer, e-mail, and Internet site logs to adequately investigate the allegations.

Schools are just now beginning to realize the need to consider computer technology as an essential part of any thorough investigation. When schools wait a period of days or weeks to seize an employee's computer, they are likely to lose key evidence of misconduct. In other cases that do not directly involve the computer as the source of the misconduct, schools may not realize the importance of examining the employee's computer to see if it contains relevant evidence.

Schools should begin investigations with a concrete plan. Part of that plan should be to assess the role technology may have played in the alleged offense. If evidence could be on a computer, the computer should be seized immediately and its data reviewed. Properly crafted policies and employee notifications, as discussed above, should remove any legal obstacles to such seizures. Computer hard drives generally retain a great deal of data that the user believes has been deleted. In order to find all data that may possibly be found, schools may need to hire a trained expert.

First Amendment Issues

Most of the legal issues involving computers in the schools stem from the use of computers for communications such as e-mail, Web browsing, and chat sessions. Wherever there is communication of ideas, the First Amendment right of free speech is likely to come into play. The Internet as a whole has been deemed by the Supreme Court of the United States to be a forum where the highest degree of First Amendment protection applies. In the landmark case of *Reno v. ACLU*, the court said, "[A]ny person with a phone line can become a town crier with a voice that resonates farther than it could from any soapbox."[15] If the Internet is a constitutionally protected marketplace of ideas—an electronic town square—can schools restrict teacher expression that is carried over the Internet?

Teacher Speech

Just because government cannot restrict freedom of speech on the Internet does not mean schools cannot restrict expression by school employees on the school's computer systems. School employees retain the right under the First Amendment to speak freely on matters of public concern, but the school may restrict the speech of an employee when the employee is acting strictly out of personal interest.[16] A matter of public concern would include, for example, an issue about the quality of teaching, administration of the school district, and even matters of educational philosophy. That's as opposed to a private concern, which might be a person griping about her or his own salary or the discipline received in response to a specific incident. Thus, the school may prohibit or punish inappropriate employee communications on the school's computer system when the speech is not on a matter of public concern. Also, the same right to regulate speech applies when teachers are implementing the board-approved curriculum or otherwise acting in their official capacity.

The more difficult question involves the regulation of speech on a matter of public concern that is protected by the First Amendment. Whether employees will have enforceable free speech rights on the school's computer communication systems will depend primarily on whether the school has permitted the system to function as an open or limited open forum for expression of ideas by teachers. As an example, consider a case where teachers become active in local school board elections, with the goal of ousting the current members of the board and electing new members. Teachers begin sending mass e-mails to other staff and even to many parents whose e-mail addresses they have collected. The mass e-mail provokes many e-mail responses and a wide-ranging e-mail discussion of the school board's performance. If the school has no clear policy on employee use of the e-mail system, and it has been used extensively by teachers for expression of views on political, educational, and other issues, the authority of the school administration to restrict this political activity will be in doubt. The courts frown upon content-based restrictions on speech. By failing to establish rules for use of the school computer system beforehand, the school has permitted an open forum to exist, and it will be hard-pressed to ban discussion of particular subjects or views after-the-fact—no matter how distasteful to district officials.

If, on the other hand, the school has a very clear policy stating that the electronic communications systems are to be used by employees only for the performance of their jobs, and all other uses are prohibited, and the system is not a forum for the expression of personal opinions on any subject, then the administration will be in a much stronger position to direct the staff to discontinue the political activity on the system. The action will not be based on the point of view expressed or the particular subject matter of the communication but solely on the fact it is not a work-related use of the system.

In addition, some state laws (*e.g.* California, Iowa, and Wisconsin) are explicit in prohibiting the use of public equipment to assist in political campaigns, ballot issues, or other political activities.

Restrictions on Teacher Internet Access

Just as the school may restrict electronic communication by school staff to work-related purposes, it may also restrict World Wide Web research to work-related purposes. A June 2000 decision by the 4th U.S. Circuit Court of Appeals in Virginia says schools may restrict the scope and nature of a teacher's Web research (whether elementary-secondary or higher education), and academic freedom issues do not apply. In *Urofsky v. Gilmore*[17], the 4th Circuit Court ruled that a statute barring all state employees from using state computers to display on their screen, download, print, or store files having "sexually explicit content" does not violate the Constitution's First Amendment freedom of speech.

The plaintiffs in the case were professors at state colleges and universities who claimed the law unconstitutionally restricted access to material they needed for their academic pursuits. The Court reasoned that the professors are state employees, and their right to receive material in that role is limited. The opinion asserts that, "the state, as an employer, undoubtedly possesses greater authority to restrict the speech of its employees than it has as a sovereign to restrict the speech of the citizenry as a whole." Since the need for Web access involves an employee (university professor) in his capacity at work, the speech cannot possibly be considered "a matter of public concern," and the extra protections that usually go along with public speech are withheld.

The 4th Circuit noted that the act allows the university professors to pursue any research they please if they get prior permission. The law contains an exception for a "bona fide, agency-approved research project or other agency-approved undertaking." The Court addressed at some length the concept of academic freedom and concluded that professors had no individual, constitutional right to academic freedom that would prevent the state from regulating their use of state-owned computers.

In addition to curricular control, the public schools in general have a greater obligation to protect minor children from access to inappropriate material. If teachers download such material, the risk is increased that children will be exposed to it. Therefore, it makes sense to apply the same rules that districts employ to restrict student access to inappropriate materials to teachers and other employees as well.

Children's Internet Protection Act

The recently enacted Children's Internet Protection Act (CIPA) requires schools to restrict not only student access to the Internet (see Chapter 1), but also employee access. The law applies to:

- all school units that receive discounted rates for Internet connection service under the federal E-rate program;[18]

- all school units that receive federal funding to purchase computers used to access the Internet, or to pay for direct costs associated with accessing the Internet under Title III of the Elementary and Secondary Education Act of 1965.[19]

The provisions for recipients of E-rate discounts and those for recipients of Title III funds are generally the same but differ in some details.

Under the CIPA, all covered schools must have an Internet safety policy for all users, including adults, that includes the operation of a "technology protection measure" with regard to all computers with Internet access. The "measure" must protect against adult (as well as child) access to visual depictions that are obscene or constitute child pornography. This differs from the filtering required for minors in that it does not require schools to prevent adult access to materials that are "harmful to minors." Adults may have access to material that is deemed "harmful to minors" although, as a practical matter, installation of software that distinguishes this category of material on certain adults-only computers is not likely to occur.

"Obscene" and "child pornography" are terms that are specifically defined by federal statutes. Materials fitting within these definitions are not protected as speech by the First Amendment with regard to adults. Materials that are "harmful to minors," on the other hand, may be protected "speech" with respect to adults in some contexts. As discussed above, however, in the context of school computer use, with proper policies in place, employees do not have free speech rights.

Rules and Policies for Employee Use of School Computers

Schools should establish a clear set of separate rules concerning staff use of their school-provided computers and the school's network and Internet connection. Such rules will reduce misuse of the systems and will provide the foundation for discipline should misuse occur.

Schools have taken a variety of approaches to regulating staff/employee use of computers and the Internet. In the rush to implement acceptable use policies for students, some schools have neglected to adopt any policies (or well-thought out, comprehensive policies) concerning employee use of computers. Others have incorporated staff into a single general acceptable use policy.

Can a District Halt Electronic Political Action without Violating Free Speech Rights?

If the school has a very clear policy stating that electronic communication systems are to be used by employees only for the performance of their jobs, no other use is permitted, and the system is not a forum for the unrestrained expression of opinion, then a district can direct the staff to discontinue any political activity on the system.

Clearly, rules for employee use of school computers should be promulgated and disseminated. In this writer's view, it makes more sense to have a separate policy for employees who are adults and who are likely to be held to different standards than students. An annotated sample policy is contained in appendices. A policy for employees might address the following issues:

Personal use

The school district may provide that district computers, networks, and Internet connection shall be used only for purposes related to the schools and the performance of the employees work, and no personal use of any kind is permitted. This would prohibit personal e-mail, creation of personal word processing documents, personal Web surfing, and all other personal activities. It would also prevent all kinds of solicitation that is not school-sanctioned—political, religious, commercial, nonprofit—without regard to the content of the solicitation.

The advantage of this approach is that it sets a clear, bright-line rule that all employees should understand, and, if obeyed, it will protect the school district's computers from inappropriate uses. Enforcement will be very difficult, and employees are likely to violate the rule on a regular basis, but the rule will provide the school the authority to act decisively when it becomes aware of violations. Yet, school districts with bargaining units should be aware that an outright ban could in some circumstances be considered an unfair labor practice. For example, the Office of General Counsel for the National Labor Relations Board (NLRB) found in *Pratt & Whitney* [20] that a company's prohibition of all non-business use of electronic e-mail was overly broad and facially (i.e., clearly) unlawful. The General Counsel concluded that the employer could offer no evidence of special circumstances that made the rule necessary to maintain production or discipline.

Contrast this finding with the same NLRB General Counsel's opinion in IRIS-USA [21] that found that the same sort of prohibition was proper. The distinction, the opinion says, is that employees in this particular case performed manual production and distribution work and did not have general access to computers and e-mail.

An alternative approach that recognizes and permits some personal use might be:

> School computers, networks, and Internet access are provided to support the educational mission of the school. They are to be used primarily for school-related purposes. Incidental personal use of school computers must not interfere with the employee's job performance, must not violate any of the rules contained in this policy or the Student Acceptable Use Policy, and must not damage the school's hardware, software, or computer communications systems.

Other alternatives are contained in the annotated sample policy found in the appendices.

Copyright

The policy should contain a rule against illegal publication or copying of copyrighted material and a statement that employees will be held personally liable for any of their own actions that violate copyright laws (See also Chapter 4).

Confidentiality

Employees should be directed not to transmit confidential information concerning students or others and to use care to protect against negligent disclosure of such information. Because of concerns about confidentiality in electronic communications, some schools construct or purchase special secure systems that safeguard information in a heightened way.

Privacy

As discussed above, the policy should provide that all data stored or transmitted on school computers can and will be monitored, and employees have no right to privacy with regard to such data.

Harassment

The employee policy should remind employees that school policies against sexual harassment and other forms of discriminatory harassment apply equally to communication on school computer systems.

Misuse of networks, hardware, or software

The policy may provide that damage caused by intentional misuse of equipment will be charged to the user.

Safeguard accounts and passwords

Employees should be reminded they are responsible for safeguarding their own passwords, and they will be held accountable for the consequences of intentional or negligent disclosure of this information.

Illegal uses

Local policies should attempt to identify categories of illegal uses to put employees on notice.

Advertising

School employees are often involved in outside businesses, and they may find it tempting to advertise or solicit on the school's e-mail system for such products as Amway, Avon, or Tupperware or such services as an investment co-op. Such advertising can unnecessarily clutter the school's e-mail system and will probably be unwelcome to most recipients. The best way to prevent this is for the school district to adopt a policy that prohibits advertising and solicitation on school computers. The policy should be broad enough to prohibit an employee from sending messages from a home or other outside computer to school district e-mail users.

Fund-raising, nonprofit, or charitable solicitation

Another common use of e-mail is to solicit or announce fund-raising events for nonprofit organizations. Schools may decide they will allow such use, perhaps with prior approval, or they will forbid it. However, districts should be aware that if they permit fund-raising activity to take place, they may not be able to bar particular solicitations just because they disagree with the cause. Whether the use is permitted or not, the issue should be addressed in the employee use policy.

Representing personal views as those of the school district

Any e-mail sent from the school computer is likely to contain a return address identifying the school district. Thus, sending an e-mail from the school is analogous to an employee using school letterhead. Accordingly employees should be put on notice to be careful not to have their own statements mistakenly attributed to the district.

Downloading or loading software or applications without permission from the administrator

There is an enormous quantity and variety of free software available on the Internet. In addition to viruses that could infect the school's systems, the cumulative effect of widespread downloading to the school's computers, in terms of degradation of performance and additional maintenance, can be significant. School districts can prohibit outside software, or place restrictions upon it, such as getting pre-approval from the technology coordinator or system administrator.

The Role of the Technology Coordinator or System Administrator

In many schools, the technology coordinator knows far more about computers and school networks than any school administrator. This person is more likely to discover violations of use policies than any other person. It is important that the duties of the technology coordinator match coherently with the acceptable use policy. Assuming this person is not in a position to handle disciplinary matters, the coordinator may play an important role in the reporting and investigation of violations. The coordinator may be required to report all violations of the policy to a particular administrator, to preserve evidence of the violation in digital form and/or hard copy, and to assist the administrator in further investigation involving the school computer systems.

The technology coordinator should also be given clear direction concerning confidentiality. This person will necessarily have access to information—such as student information protected by the Family Educational Rights & Privacy Act,[22] confidential employee information, and confidential administrative communications— that he or she should not share with others. By clearly defining the individual's duties in a job description or written memorandum, the school can help to prevent mistakes resulting from lack of awareness of confidentiality concerns.

Collective Bargaining Issues

The Duty to Bargain

Most states permit school employees to bargain collectively with school boards. In general, bargaining laws require employers to negotiate about wages, hours, and working conditions. The precise scope of the duty to bargain and the exceptions to this duty, however, vary from state to state. Under general principles of collective bargaining, it is likely that certain aspects of employee use of school computers will be mandatory subjects of bargaining.

Unions may demand to bargain on such issues as union use of the school e-mail system, employee privacy rights, use of e-mail for disciplinary purposes, personal use of the school's computer systems, and liability for damage to the system. Because state laws on collective bargaining vary and because these issues are new to collective bargaining, it is not possible to generalize about whether school boards have a duty to negotiate concerning specific issues. School board negotiators should not be too quick to concede the negotiability of these issues, however, and should consult with their attorneys or bargaining consultants concerning theories that would support a refusal to bargain. Once provisions securing employee and union rights to school computer use are ensconced in contracts, they will become very difficult to remove.

Union Use of Computer Systems

Teacher collective bargaining agreements often contain provisions allowing the union and teachers to have access to school mailboxes, interoffice mail delivery, bulletin boards, and telephones. Unions are often permitted use of school equipment, particularly copiers, for union business. Unions are increasingly seeking access to the power of computers and computer communications, and they can be expected to attempt to bargain for access to and use of the school's computer systems. E-mail can provide unions with instant access to all of their members. Through the use of mass e-mails, union leaders can quickly galvanize their entire membership with regard to particular issues. E-mail also can improve their communications with their professional representatives.

School board negotiators should consider all the implications before agreeing to union use of the school's computer systems. Permitting union use of the school's computer systems will increase system traffic, thereby increasing the risk of network problems related to such traffic. Staff members receiving union-related e-mails at work can be distracted or even disrupted. In addition, allowing unions unfettered use of the computer communications provides them a very powerful communications medium that may be used in a manner adverse to the school board's interests and goals. Because the nominal cost of allowing union use of existing systems may be negligible, school board negotiators may be quick to agree to such access. Such access should have great value to the union, however, and at the very least school boards should expect to get something of value in return for agreeing to it.

If collective bargaining does not govern board-union relations, districts should seek to clearly define whether union use of e-mail is permitted. Employers must be very careful about prohibiting or penalizing use of the school e-mail for union organizing or other concerted activities. The National Labor Relations Board has ruled that an employer may not ban union access to an e-mail system where employees were allowed to use the system for other personal purposes. Although federal labor law does not apply to local public schools, state public employee bargaining laws are often modeled on the federal law and interpreted in a similar way. It is clear, at least under federal labor law, that banning union e-mail while allowing other non-business-related expression, is probably discriminatory and illegal. The

---

Considerations in Granting Labor Union Access to School District Computers

1. School boards should ponder all the implications of access before granting consent.

2. Unions could use this powerful communications medium to defy the school board's interests.

3. Because of the small financial cost of allowing unions to use existing systems, school board negotiators may be prematurely quick to agree to such use.

4. Such access has great value to unions, and at the very least school boards should expect to get something of value in return.

5. Without a collective bargaining agreement, districts must be very careful about prohibiting or penalizing use of the school e-mail for union organizing or other activities.

---

unsettled question is whether a general ban of all advocacy and solicitation on the employer's e-mail system may be applied to union activities. Unless the issue is fully covered by collective bargaining agreements, school employers should give careful thought to how they wish to address union activity in employee e-mail policies and are well advised to consult their labor relations attorney when doing so.[23]

Technology Training for Teachers

The addition of computer technologies to classrooms and libraries will be of little use if teachers do not know how to use them effectively in the educational program. As with any other new educational program or tool, effective use requires training, and schools must struggle with ways to provide efficient training to teachers. Contractual restrictions on training time may impair a district's efforts to provide adequate training. Restrictions on the number of work days, the length of days, the number of after-school sessions and requirements for outside course work may all come into play when schools seek to train teachers on making effective use of technology. Depending upon the applicable bargaining law and the existing contract, school boards may have to bargain with teachers' unions for adequate training time and/or for additional compensation for that time. In general, however, the collective bargaining implications of computer training are the same as those that apply to other mandatory teacher training. There will be pressure from unions either to provide release time or additional compensation for such additional training requirements.

Working Safely with Computers

It is now generally accepted that the use of computers, or video display terminals, can cause or aggravate certain health problems. Complaints include excessive fatigue; eye strain and irritation; blurred vision; headaches; stress; and neck, back, arm, and muscle pain. Some have also raised concerns about exposure to electromagnetic fields radiating from computers.

Heavier users are more likely to suffer from these symptoms than those who use computers only for brief periods daily, but it is reasonable to assume that as the rate of computer use by staff members increases overall, so will the incidence of symptoms attributed to such use. When staff members suffer such symptoms, they are more likely to be absent from work, and they are likely to file a greater number of workers' compensation claims for medical expenses and lost time. Proper training, supervision, and furnishings for computer users can, however, help to prevent injuries that result from improper use of computers.

The Health Risks

According to the Occupational Safety and Health Administration (OSHA) of the U.S. Department of Labor, the primary computer-related areas of health concern are as follows:[24]

Visual problems

Eye strain and irritation are among the more common complaints by people operating computers. These symptoms may be caused by improper lighting, glare from the screen, position of the screen, or materials that are difficult to read.

Fatigue and musculoskeletal problems

When computer users maintain a fixed posture over long periods of time, they may suffer muscle fatigue and, after a while, muscle pain and injury. Users are also at risk for various musculoskeletal disorders such as carpal tunnel syndrome and tendinitis. These problems can cause chronic pain or even permanent disability.

Such problems can be especially acute for students because of the poor posture used while working on a computer. According to a study published in a 1998 article in *Computers in the Schools*, "some elementary school computers are set up without accommodation for healthy typing postures, and that could put children at risk of developing the painful repetitive stress injuries that have affected office workers in recent years." [25]

The study, conducted by Cornell University researcher Shawn Oates, is based on the observations of 95 researchers who watched elementary school children from 11 schools as they worked at computers in classrooms and computer labs. The study found "striking misfits" when comparing the size of the children and the computer workstations they used.

Radiation

Some have expressed concern that radiation emissions from computers could pose a health risk, particularly for pregnant women. According to OSHA, there is no conclusive evidence that the low levels of radiation emitted from computers pose a health risk to operators. The issue is still being researched and studied.

In November 2000, OSHA issued its final ergonomics standard requiring employers to implement ergonomics programs and to address jobs where musculoskeletal disorders occur. The standards have been more than 10 years in the making. The agency says that the standards will help protect against such maladies as repetitive motion disorders, back pain, and tendinitis. The new requirements are scheduled to take effect in October 2001 but have been met with skepticism and opposition by industry. Bush administration supporters scheduled public forums throughout the summer and have said they are considering whether to repeal or revise the standards. Also, new standards legislation has been introduced in Congress as an alternative to OSHA's 2000 proposals.

Prevention of Computer-related Injuries

Schools have a significant interest in preventing injuries and adverse symptoms of computer use in order to keep their employees healthy, to prevent absenteeism and job modifications necessitated by such conditions, and to prevent workers' compensation claims that will increase insurance rates. Certainly, clerical workers and others using keyboards and monitors for a large portion of the work day are most at risk, but other staff members, such as teachers who are increasingly using computers at work, can benefit from preventive measures.

The literature on computer operator injuries indicates that most can be prevented or minimized through training and proper use of the equipment. The design of the work station, including keyboard height and angle, monitor height, lighting, and seating can all affect the health of the user. In addition, the behavior of the user—including posture, sitting position, the introduction of variety into work routines, and taking regular breaks—will have a direct effect on the risk of symptoms.

Because environmental and behavioral factors are so pivotal in preventing injuries resulting from computer use, schools can do a lot to reduce the incidence of symptoms by arranging all workstations properly, training all users, and supervising users to ensure compliance with safety rules. Training can be provided in a variety of ways. Publications are available to instruct employers and employees on proper design and use of computer workstations. (See "Resources" section at the end of this chapter.)

On-site training is usually even more effective. Some workers' compensation providers will give free training to employees. Insurance companies may even reduce policy rates if such training is provided. The most effective method is to have the trainer visit and observe the workstation of each user. Larger school districts may train one of their own employees to provide such training in-house, including follow-up visits with computer users to ensure they are adhering to good safety practices. In addition, workplace health consultants may be hired at a fee to provide staff training.

While the training is most important for heavy computer users, all staff members who routinely use computers in their work should be given some training on safe practices. Teachers in particular are known for setting up their personal work spaces in their classrooms in unique ways. But, the school may set parameters that prevent any computer setups that increase the risk of adverse physical symptoms.

A significant benefit of implementing and maintaining a program of computer safety training is the financial savings that will result from fewer absences and workers' compensation claims. This is not to say that there are not costs involved. These costs may include the cost of training, additional furnishings required to make workstations safe, and lighting changes. While any significant expenditure will, and should, prompt a cost-benefit analysis before a purchasing decision is made, the school's investment in safety is likely to pay off in the long run.

Conclusion

Staff access to networked and Internet-connected personal computers poses a number of new challenges and wondrous opportunities for public schools. The promise of instant information access is exciting and opens brand new chances to achieve educational meaning for each child. By planning and developing appropriate rules and policies, schools should be able to meet and adjust to these challenges, and thereby to help technology make learning more productive.

Bruce W. Smith is a partner with the law firm of Drummond Woodsum & MacMahon in Portland, Maine. He has represented school districts for more than 15 years and is coauthor of the book, Maine School Law. Smith has developed a special interest in legal issues concerning electronic communications in schools and is a frequent speaker and writer on school law topics. He is an instructor for the University of Southern Maine Law School and chairman of the Maine Council of School Attorneys.

This chapter revises and updates "Legal Considerations in Regulating Employee Use of School Technology," by Bruce W. Smith. Legal Issues & Education Technology: A School Leader's Guide (1999)), Alexandria, VA: National School Boards Association.

RESOURCES

Electronic Resources

Computer Workstation Ergonomics – from the Centers for Disease Control and Prevention; guidelines to help prevent injuries, evaluation checklists, advice on exercises, and other preventive measures.
http://www.cdc.gov/od/ohs/Ergonomics/compergo.htm

Computer-related Repetitive Strain Injury – an overview of symptoms and preventive measures, as well as a very comprehensive list of links to other resources.
http://www.engr.unl.edu/ee/eeshop/rsi.html

Desktop Yoga – an overview and sample pages from Desktop Yoga™ (1998) by Julie T. Lusk. Breathing techniques, exercises, and wellness and stress management techniques intended to reduce discomfort and improve concentration and productivity.
http://www.relaxationstation.com/desktop.htm

Office Ergonomics – very comprehensive site devoted to workplace ergonomic issues. Includes a checklist to help identify workstation-related risk behavior. http://www.office-ergo.com/

Workstation Comfort Exercises and **Eye Safety at Video Display Terminals** – information provided on the Web pages of Western Washington University's Environmental Health and Safety office. http://www.ac.wwu.edu/~ehs/wrkstatn.htm

Working Safely with Video Display Terminals. OSHA Publication 3092. 1997 (revised). Washington, DC: U.S. Department of Labor, Occupational Safety & Health Administration. http://www.osha-slc.gov/SLTC/computerworkstation/index.html

Print Resources on Employee E-mail and Expectation of Privacy

Julia Turner Baumhart, **"The Employer's Right to Read Employee E-mail: Protecting Property or Personal Prying,"** 8 Labor Lawyer 923 (1992).

Kevin G. DeNoce, **"Internet Privacy Jurisprudence Begins to Develop,"** National Law Journal, July 21, 1997, at B11.

Thomas R. Greenberg, **"E-mail and Voice Mail: Employee Privacy and the Federal Wiretap Statute,"** 44 American U.L. Rev. 219 (1994).

Wesley College v. Pitts, 974 F.Supp. 375 (D.Del. 1997) – addresses **the "interception" of e-mail under the Electronic Communications Privacy Act**.

Endnotes

1   Donn Ritchie & Karen Boyle, *Finding the Bucks for Technology*, Learning and Leading with Technology, Vol. 26, No. 2, Oct. 1998.

2   *Id.*

3   99-2-00794-2 (Superior Court of Spokane County, Oct. 15, 1999

4   See O'Connor v. Ortega, 480 U.S. 709 (1987).

5   480 U.S. 709 (1987).

6   Pub. L. No. 99-508, 100 Stat. 1848, also 18 U.S.C. Section 2510-2522.

7   Kevin J. Baum, *E-Mail in the Workplace and the Right of Privacy*, 42 Vill. L. Rev. 1011, 1024 (May 1997).

8   18 U.S.C. Section 2511

9   135 F.Supp.2d 623 (E.D. Penn. 2001)

10   The common law consists of the body of widely accepted legal principles developed over time by judges deciding court cases, as distinguished from the Constitution, statutes, and regulations.

11   Restatement (Second) of Torts, Section 625B.

12   *McLaren v. Microsoft Corporation*, 1999 WL 339015 (Tex.App.-Dallas)

13   *Bourke v. Nissan Motor Corp.*, Cal. Super. Ct. No. YC003979 (Cal.App. 1991).

14   *Smyth v. Pillsbury Co.*, 914 F.Supp. 97 (E.D.Pa. 1996).

[15] *Reno v. ACLU*, 117 S. Ct. 2329 (1997).

[16] *Connick v. Myers*, 461 U.S. 138 (1983); Pickering v. Board of Education, 391 U.S. 563 (1968).

[17] *Urofsky v. Gilmore*, 216 F.3d 401 (4th Cir. 2000).

[18] Section 254(h) of the Telecommunications Act of 1934, 47 U.S.C. 254(h).

[19] 20 U.S.C. § 6801.

[20] 1998 WL 1112978

[21] 2000 WL 257107 (February 2000)

[22] The federal Family Educational Rights and Privacy Act restricts disclosure of personally identifiable information from a student's "educational records." An e-mail message itself may well constitute an "education record" which should be protected under the law. When a staff member communicates with another staff member concerning a student for legitimate educational purposes, that kind of information-sharing is not prohibited by FERPA. Disclosures about students to staff members who have no need for the information or especially to outside persons could violate FERPA, however. In addition, employee information transmitted electronically should also be guarded against inappropriate disclosures that may violate state employee privacy laws or common law rights of privacy.

[23] A helpful discussion of the status of federal law on this issue is contained in Robfogel, *Electronic Communication and the NLRA: Union Access and Employer Rights,* 16 Lab. Law. 231 (Fall 2000).

[24] "Working Safely with Video Display Terminals" OSHA Publication No. 3092 (1997) http://www.osha-slc.gov/SLTC/computerworkstation/index.html.

[25] Shawn Oates, Gary W. Evans, & Alan Hedge. 1998. An anthropometric and postural risk-assessment of children's school computer work environment, *Computers in Schools* 14 (3-4), 55-63.

Chapter 4

Copyright Law

Janis H. Bruwelheide, Ph.D.
Professor of Education
College of Education, Health, and Human Development
Montana State University-Bozeman

Introduction

Since the last total revision of the Copyright Act in 1976, a tremendous variety of new technologies and applications have flooded society. Think back to 1976, when several technologies and applications that we consider mainstream were not yet available. Examples are videocassette recorders, personal computers, Web browsers, CD-ROMs and DVDs, just to name a few. More than ever before, it is imperative that public school district personnel understand how to apply copyright to education. What has previously been done in classrooms now has a new meaning as the Web and Internet allow teachers and students to seek knowledge from and expand their reach to a global audience far beyond the "closed doors" of traditional classrooms.

The wonderful menu of technologies and applications presents exciting opportunities for education as students and teachers explore new horizons. Electronic technology, digital learning, and "virtual" environments have become necessities, not luxuries, in public schools. Along with the advantages, however, new technologies also present novel legal challenges. Therefore, in addition to possessing knowledge about laws that relate to collective bargaining, instruction, and discipline, public school decision makers must now also possess a basic understanding of the law of intellectual property.

This chapter will present an overview of copyright law for the non-legal school district policymaker. It will review fundamental principles of copyright law that educators are likely to encounter, and it will address some issues particular to public schools, with a focus on newer technologies. It will also outline suggestions for copyright policies and procedures.

General Principles of Copyright

A Federal Doctrine

All copyright law is federal and is specifically mentioned in the United States Constitution. Article I, Section 8, Clause 8 states:

> Congress shall have power. . . To promote the Progress of Science and useful Arts by securing for limited Times to Authors and Inventors the exclusive Right to their respective Writings and Discoveries.

The purpose of copyright law is to benefit the public good through the twin goals of *promotion* of public interest and *protection* of private rights. That is, the public is able to benefit from the fruits of the creative process though the protection granted to individual authors. Because individual creators have the right to control their products, their economic interests are protected from unfair exploitation.

Exclusive rights

Copyright law[1] gives to the owner of a creative work the exclusive right to:

- Reproduce the copyrighted work in copies or phono records;

- Create derivative works based upon the copyrighted work (e.g., to create books from movies; or musicals from books);

- Distribute copies of the copyrighted work to the public by sale, rental, lease or lending;

- Perform publicly any literary, musical, dramatic or choreographic work;

- Display publicly any sculpture, motion picture, pictorial, graphic work, or pantomime.[2]

Because copyright is a form of property, it can be sold, transferred, or licensed. For example, many copyright owners license to school districts the right to perform plays or musicals.

What can be copyrighted

Copyright law extends to "original works of authorship, fixed in any tangible medium of expression now known or later developed from which they can be perceived, reproduced or otherwise communicated, either directly or with the aid of a machine or device."[3] This statement from twenty-five years ago is very powerful since it encompasses various forms of technology. Yet, it does not provide guidance for newer technologies used in education today. Ideas cannot be copyrighted.[4] Rather, copyright protects the manner in which an idea has been expressed, which is embodied in a "work of authorship."

The law places works of authorship into the following categories:

- literary works;

- musical works, including accompanying words;

- dramatic works, including accompanying music;

- pantomimes and choreographic works;

- pictorial, graphic, and sculptural works;

- motion pictures and other audiovisual works;

- sound recordings, and

- architectural works.[5]

Example 1. What can be copyrighted?

Zora Neale is a library media specialist at Harlem High School in the Renaissance School District. Zora has devised a software program that can assist students in improving their reading comprehension skills. Zora would be able to copyright her software program. Under the law, the software program is a "literary work."

Under the Copyright Act, Zora's software program can receive copyright protection. It can be "perceived" and "reproduced" and is embodied in a tangible form.

Example 2. What can be copyrighted?

Suppose that Zora performs a demonstration lesson for members of the administration and school board. Unlike the software program, the demonstration lesson cannot be "fixed." (It is over after she has taught it.) Zora would not be able to receive copyright protection for the demonstration lesson that she has performed.[6]

Copyright protection begins from the moment that an idea has been "fixed" in a "tangible medium." It is not necessary to place any copyright notice[7] on the document or to register a work with the Copyright Office in order to receive the rights conferred by statute.[8] Therefore, neither students nor staff members should assume that a work lacks copyright protection because it is not registered with the Copyright Office. Prior to March 1989, absence of a notice often meant that works were in the public domain, but that is no longer the case. Similarly, there is no requirement to place a notice of copyright on an item in order to confer an owner's exclusive rights.

Example. Copyright protection

James, a talented eighth-grader, writes an exceptional series of poems for his English class. James clearly holds the copyright to his poetry. Zora, who wishes to publish the poetry on the school Web site, would be required to seek James's permission prior to "displaying" his poetry on the site.

Best Practice

Even though the copyright notice is not required on a work, it is a good idea to use it. Affixing the notice does several things. It clearly indicates that the work (Web page, document, CD-ROM, video) is copyrighted and by whom. Thus, it makes it harder for people to state that they did not know an item was copyrighted, and it makes it easier to locate the copyright owner to request permission or cite appropriately.

Duration of copyright protection

Copyright protection, or an owner's exclusive control, is not perpetual. One of the law's goals is to promote the public good. To promote this goal, the private right must possess specific time limits. Without such limits, the owner's control might prevent any access by the public.

The Sonny Bono Copyright Term Extension Act, S. 505 P. L. 105-298 (signed into law on October 27, 1998) extends the term of copyright protection of work created on or after January 1, 1978. For individual authors, the term of protection is life of the author plus 70 years. For corporate creators or for joint works of authorship, the term is 95 years after the date of first publication, or 120 years, which ever expires first. Once a work no longer receives copyright protection, it is considered part of the

"public domain" and may be reproduced, copied, or performed without seeking the author's permission.

Example. How long does it last?
Harriet Jacobs is the faculty advisor for drama productions at Harlem High. She wants to produce two plays: *Taming of the Shrew*, written by William Shakespeare in 1594, and *Raisin in the Sun*, written by Lorraine Hansberry in 1957. Under the Act, Harriet would not need permission to produce Shakespeare's play. However, the Hansberry work is still protected by copyright. She would have to seek permission from Hansberry's heirs.[9]

The Copyright Term Extension Act includes an exception for libraries, archives, and not-for-profit schools. These organizations may, during the last 20 years of a copyright term, "reproduce, perform, distribute, or display [a work] in facsimile or digital form" for the purposes of preservation, scholarship, or research. However, schools are restricted from taking these actions if the work is still subject to commercial exploitation, if copy can be obtained at a reasonable price, or if the copyright owner has given notice that the work cannot be used.

Copyright ownership

In most cases, the owner of a copyright is also the creator of a copyright. However, when a work is prepared by an employee within the scope of his or her employment[10] the employer, rather than the creator, retains the exclusive rights of ownership. The work is considered a "work made for hire." In such cases, the owner of the copyright may be an individual or an entity, such as a local board of education. The United States Copyright Office has stated that works such as a newspaper article written by a staff journalist for publication, a software program created by a staff programmer for a computer corporation, or a musical arrangement for a music company produced by a salaried arranger on staff would be examples of works made for hire. In general, a court will examine: whether the employee's status is related to the nature of the work that has been created; whether the work performed by the employee is related to the employer's regular business; whether the employer withholds taxes for the employee; and whether the employer has control over the employee.[11] However, employment alone is not a sufficient condition to deem something a work made for hire.[12]

Boards of Education, like other employers, have the option of granting copyrights to their employees even when the works would normally be considered works made for hire. Any such option should be clearly noted in your school board's policy. Given the current interest in developing "virtual curricula" and "virtual classes," perhaps shared ownership or royalty payments could be considered. These approaches could provide incentives for teachers to spend the considerable time required to learn online instructional techniques, understand how various software operate, and actually teach online.

Example 1. Work made for hire
Suppose that Zora's cousin, Janie, is Webmaster for Harlem High School. The position, like those of coach and class advisor, carries a stipend negotiated through the district's collective bargaining agreement. Janie designs the school's award-winning Web page. Because Janie has designed the Web page as a part of her employment, the school district would own the copyright in the Web page.

The issue of ownership of faculty-created works has never been litigated in the public school context. However, there are several items that teachers create during the ordinary course of employment that may or may not be considered works made for hire. For example:

Example 2. Work made for hire
Suppose that Benita decides to try to market the lesson plans that have brought her acclaim throughout the district. Would the Renaissance Board of Education be correct if it asserted that the plans are the property of the school board, not the individual employee?

Benita is clearly an employee of the school system and has created the lesson plans during the ordinary course of her employment. However, Benita could argue that the plans were created for her personal benefit — not to be used or endorsed by the entire school district. Unlike the computer programmer who was hired to write computer programs, or the newspaper reporter who was hired to write newspaper feature articles, Benita was not hired to write lesson plans; she was hired to teach. The following example illustrates the difference:

Example 3. Work made for hire
Suppose that Zora's demonstration lesson is videotaped by the school district's administration. The school board decides to package the tape, together with curricular materials, to market to other school districts. The Board also plans to use the tape in teacher training sessions. It is likely that the school district, not Zora, would own the tape of the lesson.[13]

This is an issue that your school board should discuss fully prior to adopting a policy on the ownership of copyrighted materials.

Fair use of copyrighted materials
In the same way that the time limits on an author's work provide access by the public *after* the term of copyright protection, the concept of fair use provides access by the public *during* the term of copyright protection. Fair use attempts to balance the author's right to control against the public's need or desire to gain access to a copyrighted work. The doctrine is codified at 17 U. S. C Section 107:

> Notwithstanding the provisions of Section 106, the fair use of a copyrighted work, for purposes such as criticism, comment, news reporting, teaching (including multiple copies for classroom use), scholarship or research is *not an infringement of copyright.* (Emphasis added)

The statute requires that four factors be applied to determine whether or not a particular use is fair:

- the purpose and character of the use, including whether such use is of a commercial nature or is for nonprofit educational purposes;

- the nature of a copyrighted work;

- the amount and substantiality of the portion used in relation to the copyrighted work as a whole, and

■ the effect of the use upon the potential market for value of a copyrighted work.[14]

The application of the fair use standards is far from an exact science. Congress has called fair use an "equitable rule of reason" with "no generally applicable definition . . . possible."[15] Therefore, it is impossible to state with certainty when a use will be considered copyright infringement or fair use. Because Congress declined to construct a blanket exception for classroom use of copyrighted works, it means that teachers, students, and school administrators are, essentially, held to the same legal standard as commercial users.[16] However, the concept of fair use has held up quite well and served the education community since 1978. Education personnel must understand the concept of fair use and learn to apply it to individual settings. Some tips are provided later in this chapter.

Discussions on the topic of fair use have helped clarify the definition of the term and resulted in guidelines. Some of these guidelines might be perceived as having a bit more weight than others simply because they have been around for a while; however **none** are part of the Copyright Act. During discussions relating to the 1976 amendments of the Copyright Act, the House Committee concluded that concrete educational guidelines based on a reasonable interpretation of the minimum standards of fair use were necessary. The Committee convened a group of educational users and copyright holders to draft a set of guidelines for educational institutions. They include: "Guidelines for Classroom Copying in Not for Profit Educational Institutions", and "Guidelines for the Educational Uses of Music". "Guidelines for Off-Air Broadcasting" were released in 1981. The complete text of these guidelines is found in Appendix 4.

How your school district can benefit from applying guidelines
While not regarded as law, the guidelines provide a quantifiable standard for applying copyright law to everyday classroom situations and can be used as proof of a school district's good faith effort to follow the law. Adherence to the guidelines is considered the least that should be done to satisfy the standard of fair use. Therefore, any school district that followed them would likely be within a safe harbor.

A school district should review copyright policies and guidelines as part of routine back-to-school preparation. School Web sites can provide a convenient way to publicize the district's position on copyright with accompanying policies and manuals that include examples. Some school boards have incorporated the guidelines into their policy statements.

Copyright infringement
An individual who violates an owner's copyright is subject to both civil and criminal penalties under the Act. Copyright owners can sue for statutory or actual (e.g., lost profits) damages in an infringement action. Additionally, they may also ask for attorneys' fees and injunctive relief to bar further infringement. Because the courts have recognized contributory infringement, school districts can be held vicariously liable for the actions of students and staff.

If an educator[17] "believed and had reasonable grounds for believing" that their copying constituted fair use he/she cannot be sued for statutory damages.[18] That does not mean, however, that the district and teacher might not be named in a suit. Consistent policies, procedures, and records are important. Educators must know the

fair use standards and when they apply. Although it has not yet been tested by the courts, it is reasonable to conclude that reliance on the fair use standards and accompanying guidelines will constitute reasonable belief and action by an educator. The Act specifically notes that instrumentalities of a state, (such as a local board of education) cannot claim sovereign immunity for copyright infringement actions.[19]

Exemptions to the Copyright Law

Public education enjoys three important exemptions under the copyright law: face-to-face teaching; educational broadcasting, and nonprofit performances. Unlike the fair use standards, the exemptions are relatively simple to understand without the benefit of guidelines. The exceptions work well in a traditional teaching setting but do not translate well to electronic distance learning teaching environments.

Face-to-Face Teaching Activities

Section 110 (1) of the Copyright Act excludes school performances from a copyright owner's control over the public performance or display of a work. An owner's copyright is not infringed when there is a:

> Performance or display of a work by instructors or pupils in the course of face-to-face teaching activities of a nonprofit educational institution, in a classroom or similar place devoted to instruction, unless in the case of a motion picture or other audiovisual work, the performance or the display of individual images, is given by means of a copy that was not lawfully made under this title, and that the person responsible for the performance knew or had reason to believe was not lawfully made.[20]

Under this exemption, a teacher may read, perform or display a copyrighted work, as long as the conditions are met. First, the activity must take place "face-to-face." Although use of "devices for amplifying sound and for projecting visual images" is permitted, the instructor and pupils must be present in the same building or general area. According to Congress, this exemption is intended to exclude broadcasting or other transmissions from an outside location into classrooms.

Next, the lesson must be taught by "instructors." Congress included guest lecturers in this definition, but specifically excluded "performance by actors, singers or instrumentalists brought in from outside the school to put on a program."[21] Last, the instruction must occur in a "classroom or similar place devoted to instruction" for students. Therefore, "performances in an auditorium during a school assembly, graduation ceremony, class play or sporting event, where the audience is not confined to the members of a particular class, would fall outside the scope" of the exemption.[22]

Instructional Broadcasting

Section 110 of the Act also exempts certain instructional broadcasts from copyright infringement. Specifically, Section 110(2) states that the performance of a nondramatic literary or musical work or display of a work by or in the course of a

transmission[23] is not an infringement of copyright.

Unlike the exemption for face-to-face teaching, the instructional broadcasting exemption limits the types of copyrighted works that can be used. Nondramatic literary or musical works would exclude an opera, musical comedy, or motion picture. An owner's permission would be required in order to transmit these works.

Moreover, the performance or display must occur in a specific context. First, the statute states that it must be part of the regular systematic instructional activities of a governmental body or a nonprofit educational institution. Secondly, the performance must be directly related and of material assistance to the teaching content of the transmission. Any such transmission must be primarily (rather than solely) for reception in classrooms. Therefore, broadcasts that can be received by persons other than students are permissible. Lastly, the transmission must be received by officers or employees of a governmental body as part of their official duties or by persons who, because of their special circumstances or disabilities are unable to attend regular classrooms. For example, students who receive home and hospital instruction as well as employees who participate in staff development activities would fall into this

Excerpts of Legislative History Concerning Adoption of the 1976 Act

(testimony on fair use provisions affecting hearing-impaired students)

"... Also in consultation with section 107, the committee's attention has been directed to the unique educational needs and problems of the approximately 50,000 deaf and hearing-impaired students in the United States, and the inadequacy of both public and commercial television to serve their educational needs. It has been suggested that, as long as clear-cut constraints are imposed and enforced, the doctrine of fair use is broad enough to permit the making of an off-the-air fixation of a television program within a nonprofit educational institution for the deaf and hearing impaired, the reproduction of a master and a work copy of a captioned version of the original fixation, and the performance of the program from the work copy within the confines of the institution. In identifying the constraints that would have to be imposed within an institution in order for these activities to be considered as fair use, it has been suggested that the purpose of the use would have to be noncommercial in every respect, and educational in the sense that it serves as part of a deaf or hearing-impaired student's learning environment within the institution, and that the institution would have to insure that the master and work copy would remain in the hands of a limited number of authorized personnel within the institution, would be responsible for assuring against its unauthorized reproduction or distribution, or its performance or retention for other than educational purposes within the institution. Work copies of captioned programs could be shared among institutions for the deaf abiding by the constraints specified. Assuming that these constraints are both imposed and enforced, and that no other factors intervene to render the use unfair, the committee believes that the activities described could reasonably be considered fair use under section 107."

Source: Excerpted from the *Congressional Record*, September 22, 1976.

category. This section of the Act is problematic for distance learning course providers since it prohibits transmission of certain media via satellite, the Web, or interactive television, for example.

Nonprofit Performances

The Act excludes nonprofit performances from copyright control when: the work performed is a nondramatic literary or musical work, the work is not transmitted to the public, and there is no payment of a fee for the performance to the performers or promoters. Last, the exclusion provides that no admission charge must be assessed, or that the proceeds collected must be used exclusively for educational, religious or charitable purposes and not for private financial gain.

Congress's purpose in limiting monetary gain was to prevent free use of copyrighted material under the guise of charity where fees or percentages are paid. However, the legislative history specifically noted that school performances, where teachers were paid annual salaries, would not be considered payment of a fee to performers. For example, a school band concert, where the band director receives a stipend for her work, would not be subject to copyright control as long as the other conditions of the section are met.

Copyright in the Digital Age

The Digital Millennium Copyright Act of 1998

On October 27, 1998, President Clinton signed into law the Digital Millennium Copyright Act of 1998 (DMCA). Although the Act attempts to make the law relevant to digital technology, the DMCA does not substantially alter the sections of the statute that apply to the educational community. For example, fair use as it appears in Section 107, remains unchanged.[24] Section 110(2) dealing with transmission was not clarified for the distance learning community.

The Act directed the Register of Copyrights, within six months of the signing of the Act, to recommend to Congress how to promote distance learning through digital technologies. The Copyright Office issued its *Report on Distance Education* in May, 1999. However, as of May, 2001, no additional legislation of interest to schools had resulted from the Register's recommendations. In spring of 2001, S. 487, the Technology, Education, and Copyright Harmonization Act of 2001, proposed adoption of recommendations enumerated in the *Report on Distance Education.* The complete text of the report can be accessed on the Copyright Office Web site, which is included in the chapter resource list.

Recommendations on Distance Education by the U.S. Copyright Office

The Copyright Office issued its *Report on Distance Education** in May, 1999. Recommendations for changes and clarification to the Copyright statute were based, in part, on testimony and statements from users as well as copyright owners.

In general, recommendations were made to:

1. expand the scope of the law and related rights to meet distance learning needs and applications;

2. allow displays and performances in the context of "mediated instruction";

3. clarify and expand the transmission requirement in 110(2);

4. increase safeguards for copyright owners;

5. permit retention of a copy of the course for student access during the course term; and

6. continue the application of fair use standards to distance learning activities.

* http://www.loc.gov/copyright

Fair Use of Digital Technologies

Although Congress declined to determine specifically how fair use standards should apply to the digital age, the Conference on Fair Use (CONFU) was convened to study how fair use standards could be adapted to the digital environment.[25] After almost three years of work and discussion by CONFU participants, Bruce Lehman, Commissioner of Patents and Trademarks stated publicly in April, 1997 that proposed guidelines negotiated by participants in the CONFU process had **not achieved** consensus support. Thus, none of the proposed guidelines made it past the comment and endorsement proceedings, and no official guidelines resulted from CONFU negotiations. The Conference, which was initially composed of forty groups and later grew to over ninety organizations, proposed guidelines for use of copyrighted materials in the nonprofit educational arena. CONFU produced four sets of proposed guidelines: *Fair Use Guidelines for Educational Multimedia,*[26] *Educational Fair Use Guidelines for Distance Learning, Statement on the Use of Copyrighted Computer Programs (Software) in Libraries,* and *Guidelines for Digital Images.*[27]

The proponents of the multimedia guidelines indicated that their guidelines were well developed and had a lot of support. However, the multimedia guidelines have been opposed by several prominent educational organizations.[28] The proposed guidelines are certainly worth consideration, but it must be noted that, generally copyright owners believed that all the guidelines were too generous and that users already had enough breaks. By contrast, users thought the guidelines were too restrictive and relinquished too many privileges that the current fair use test provides. The full text of the abovementioned guidelines proposed by CONFU is included in Appendix 5.

In the absence of official guidelines, what should school district officials do? The best alternative is to develop an understanding of fair use standards, review the proposed guidelines, and decide which provide the "best fit" for individual districts. Clear policies and procedures, as well as training, will be helpful.

Specific Digital Technology: Software

Software is protected by the Copyright Act as a literary work. As such, an owner retains the right to control its copying[29] and distribution. Unlike a book or play, however, the fair use of software is almost impossible to quantify. That is, it is rare that only portions of a software program can be used. Therefore, software owners generally issue licenses to individuals. These licenses have specific conditions and usually limit the number of terminals or the site where the software may be used. Because software is protected by the copyright law, your school district may be able to limit its liability by:

■ prohibiting staff and students from copying software licensed to the school system;

■ prohibiting staff and students from loading personal software on equipment owned by the school district;

■ ' having an audit process;

■ requiring staff and students to adhere to the school district's software licenses, and strictly enforcing rules against violators.

SAMPLE POLICY STATEMENT

USE OF COPYRIGHTED MATERIALS

The Board of Education of Renaissance County hereby affirms that respect for personal property, whether tangible or intangible, is vital to maintaining a stable learning and work environment.

Students and employees of the school district are expected to follow copyright law and the copyright procedures established by the Superintendent. Any willful infringement will be punished in accordance with the student disciplinary code and employee disciplinary procedure. Students and staff members who willfully infringe the copyrights of others will be reported to the appropriate authorities and may be subject to criminal or civil penalties.

The Board of Education hereby directs the Superintendent of Schools to implement regulations consistent with this policy.

OWNERSHIP OF PRODUCTS

Unless there is a specific agreement to the contrary, products created within the scope of employment relationship shall be the property of the Board of Education. Student work, unless created while the student is working for the school district, are the property of the individual student. Unless a student gives specific direction to the contrary, the school district will display notable student work created during the same school term or school year in educational contexts (e.g., posting on school bulletin board or at a school show). In the opinion of the Board of Education, such limited educational posting constitutes fair use.

This point has never been litigated. It is an attempt to avoid asking for permission from students prior to displaying student work. Because it is unlikely that student work will have any economic impact, it is unlikely that limited posting for educational purposes will constitute infringement. However, you should discuss this issue fully with your school attorney.

It should be noted that software licenses may be negotiable to fit a district's needs if time is taken to do so before purchase. District personnel could consider beforehand possible uses that might be desired and ask for these as a "bundle" (retaining authority to use it in that specific way) when talking with software publishers.

Policy Considerations for Your School Board

School districts can reduce chances of litigation by requesting permission for use of copyrighted materials.[30] However, this method can be costly, time consuming, and inefficient. Publishers generally respond within four to six weeks, and few instructors have the luxury of such an extended period of time. However, if materials are to be used in a production or incorporated into products to be distributed in alternative formats such as CD-ROM, or a public Web page, the inconvenience is certainly worth the effort. Often a phone call to the right person, followed by a fax documenting the request and response, is all that is needed and can expedite the matter. Districts could develop a simple process for doing so and establish a recordkeeping system. Form letters are not necessarily the best approach since the request has to reach the correct person. The publisher's or producer's Web page may contain needed information.

In discussing the application of fair use standards, relevant guidelines, and ways to reduce exposure for copyright infringement, a school board should:

- Carefully review current use of copyrighted materials in the classroom. Does your school board have a policy on the use of copyrighted materials? Are staff members aware of their liability and penalities?

- Consider designating an individual to coordinate copyright requests for the school district.

- Train staff on the basic requirements of intellectual property law with a focus on copyright for teachers and students.

- Assure that staff understand how to apply the fair use standards and balance them with guidelines in order to see which fits their needs best. Remember that **the guidelines are not part of the law**; CONFU "guidelines" did not receive the necessary consensus or legislative support.

- Consult with school board counsel and have copyright policies and procedures reviewed prior to adoption.

- Establish clear standards for the use of copyrighted materials in the classroom, in multimedia productions, performances, distance learning applications, and the Web environment.

- Disseminate widely any copyright policy[31] or procedure that is adopted.

Policy Content Suggestions

The section below presents an overview of copyright policy content. Policies need not be lengthy. The policy is best kept concise and should be accompanied by a manual and appendices section containing additional information such as guidelines, sample permission letters, examples of what is permissible and what is not, and permission contact, if desired. The policy (and manual, if developed) should be distributed to everyone likely to use or duplicate copyrighted materials. Training about the policy should be conducted and then reviewed periodically. The policy must be scrutinized by counsel and adopted by the school board.

The written policy should contain the following:

- a statement that the school board intends to abide by copyright laws, patent laws, and accompanying guidelines, and that makes clear that the employees and district will work within required parameters

- a statement that prohibits copying not specifically allowed by law, fair use, license agreement, or permission of the copyright holder

- a statement that places liability for willful infringement upon the person requesting or duplicating the work and that makes clear that no institutional support will be given to an employee who violates the parameters

- a statement that identifies a copyright contact person for the district (use title not name). This person should have the authority to provide enforcement, education, and advice concerning copyright. Paperwork should be centralized with the individual, and he or she should serve as liaison to district counsel.

Tips for Managing Copyright in a Changing Environment

1. Develop a copyright policy that is reasonable. Accompany it with examples. Have the policy reviewed by counsel and adopted by the governing body.

2. Provide employee training concerning copyright.

3. Learn how to balance and apply the fair use standards and guidelines and do so! Educators really have lots of leeway, and it could become a "use it or lose it" situation.

4. Remember that one can always request permission outside the parameters from the copyright owner. Make it easier by having a request form for phone, fax, and mail, and keep those records. Address query to the appropriate person.

5. Be aware of the permissions help now available on the Web. (See chapter resources.)

6. Give copyright credit on copies and productions or products and use proper citation techniques. Teach students to do the same.

7. Be sensitive to the setting in which copyrighted material will be used. For example material used in a traditional classroom is given more leeway than material used in a distance learning environment or a public performance.

8. Help teachers and students learn how to locate public domain materials widely available on CD-ROM and the Web.

9. Think about requisite rights that might be needed from copyright owners before producing a product.

10. Make sure that students learn to respect the intellectual property of others,[31] and teach proper use of copyrighted materials and citation of sources.

■ a statement that informs employees of the school board's intent to place appropriate notices on/near all devices capable of copying materials in libraries (whether supervised or not). Self-service photocopy machines, video recorders, CD-ROM burners, etc. will be included. (Note: Section 108 of the Copyright Act has several provisions unique to libraries, and the DMCA added some privileges and requirements.)

■ a statement indicating that adequate records will be maintained (*e.g.*, permissions, requests, license agreements, etc.).

CONCLUSION

The technology and information explosion presents exciting opportunities and challenging situations for public education. Teachers and students have a wonderful menu of content, information, and technology applications at their disposal. Public school policymakers have the opportunity to shape the minds of a generation that will propel society throughout the next millennium. While the legal issues that accompany these new technologies are, in many cases, undecided, this should not prevent the careful board of education from meeting the challenges that lie ahead.

Dr. Janis H. Bruwelheide is a professor in the Department of Education in the College of Education, Health, and Human Development at Montana State University-Bozeman. Her publications include The Copyright Primer: A Handbook (co-published by the American Library Association and the National Education Association in 1995 and updated in 1998) and several book chapters and articles on copyright, distance learning, and technology. Dr. Bruwelheide is the project director for BATE: Borderless Access to Training and Education, a national distance learning demonstration project funded by the FIPSE LAAP program for the U.S. Department of Education (http://www.bate.montana.edu).

This chapter revises and updates "Copyright in the School Domain," by Margaret-Ann Howie, in Legal Issues & Education Technology: A School Leader's Guide (1999), Alexandria, VA: National School Boards Association.

RESOURCES

If your school district decides to designate a staff person to coordinate copyright questions and concerns, the following resources will provide helpful information:

Print Resources

Bruwelheide, Janis H. 1995 (updated for 1998). *Copyright primer: A handbook for librarians and educators.* 2nd ed., Washington, DC: American Library Association and National Education Association.

Nimmer on copyright. The most comprehensive treatise available (ten volumes). This is a good library resource for your school district's legal counsel.

Gorman, Robert, and Jane Ginsburg. 1997. *Copyright for the nineties: Cases and materials.* 4th ed. N. p.: Lexis Law Publishing.

Howie, Margaret-Ann F. 1997. *Copyright issues in schools: Learn how to protect yourself and your school from violating copyright law.* N. p.: LRP Publishing.

Talab, R. S. 1999. *Commonsense copyright: A guide for educators and librarians.* 2nd ed. N. p.: McFarland.

Electronic Resources

American Library Association's Washington Office Copyright Page
http://www.ala.org/washoff/copyright.html

United States Copyright Office, Library of Congress – extensive information on copyright law, pending legislation, compliance issues, and links to resources for authors, publishers, and educators. PDFs of several Copyright Office publications are available, including *Reproduction of Copyrighted Works by Educators and Librarians* (Circular 21, 1998).
http://www.loc.gov/copyright

Report on Copyright and Digital Distance Education. 1999, May. Washington, DC: U.S. Copyright Office, Library of Congress.
http://www.loc.gov/copyright/disted/

Lehman, Bruce A. 1998, November. *The Conference on Fair Use: Final report to the commissioner on the conclusion of the Conference on Fair Use.* Washington, DC: U.S. Patent and Trademark Office.
http://www2.uspto.gov/web/offices/dcom/olia/confu/

The University of Texas System Crash Course in Copyright. 2000. Copyright Management Center, Office of the General Counsel, University of Texas System. This Web site explains fair use and the educational exemptions in a clear and easily understood way. Users should remember, however, that much of what is done on the higher education level is not applicable to public education.
http://www.utsystem.edu/OGC/IntellectualProperty/cprtindx.htm#top

The Copyright Website – This site, which was created by attorney Benedict Mahoney, has a helpful fair use test and extensive information particularly useful for electronic technologies.
http://www.benedict.com/

Legal Information Institute, Cornell Law School – highly regarded source of information on recent and pending court decisions; federal and state codes; opinions; state and federal law; directories of law schools and lawyers; and more.
http://www.law.cornell.edu/

A Guide to Copyright for Music Librarians – sponsored by the Legislation Committee of the Music Library Association. Contains links and information related to music and copyright, as well as more general copyright resources.
http://www.musiclibraryassoc.org/Copyright/copyhome.htm

Copyright and Fair Use – administered by Stanford University Libraries, this site includes primary materials (statutes, opinions, regulations, etc.), current legislation, information on cases and issues, Internet resources, and an overview of copyright law.
http://fairuse.stanford.edu

When Works Pass into the Public Domain (1999, October) – This University of North Carolina Web page contains Professor Laura Gasaway's table that helps determine when works pass into the public domain.
http://www.unc.edu/~unclng/public-d.htm

Endnotes

1 Copyright law is codified in Title 17 of the United States Code.

2 17 U.S.C. Section 106.

3 17 U.S.C. Section 102(a).

4 17 U.S.C. Section 102(b) "In no case does copyright protection for an original work of authorship extend to any idea, procedure, process, system, method of operation, concept, principle, or discovery, regardless of the form in which it is explained, illustrated or embodied in such work." Ideas, on the other hand, can be patented.

5 17 U.S.C. Section 102

6 A recording of Zora's demonstration lesson, however, could receive copyright protection.

7 The standard notice of copyright consists of the copyright symbol, or the word "Copyright" or the abbreviation "Copr."; the year of the first publication of the work, and the name of the owner of the copyright. 17 U.S.C. Section 401.

8 17 U.S.C. Section 102(a).

9 Professor Laura Gassaway, University of North Carolina, has written a helpful table to determine whether a work has passed into the public domain. It is found at: <http://www.unc.edu/~unclng/public-d.htm>

10 17 U.S.C. Section 101

11 *See, generally,* <u>Community for Creative Non-Violence v. Reid</u>, 490 U.S. 730 (1989), for a discussion of these factors.

12 *See, e.g.,* <u>Newark v. Beasley</u>, 883 F. Supp. 3 (D.NJ. 1995) (police officer who created an anti-violence curriculum as a result of his lectures on behalf of the police department owned the copyright in the curriculum.)

13 <u>Quintanilla v. Texas Television, Inc.</u>, 139 F.3d 494 (5th Cir. 1998)

14 17 U.S.C. Section107(1) to (4)

15 H.Rep.94-1476, at 65. Courts, too, have stated their inability to apply the fair use standards mechanically: "The fair use doctrine permits courts to avoid rigid application of the copyright statute when, on occasion, it would stifle the very creativity which that law is designed to foster." <u>Stewart v. Abend</u>, 495 U.S. 207, 236 (1990). See, also, <u>Campbell v. Acuff-Rose Music</u>, 114 S.Ct. 1164 (1994) (parody might be within the bounds of fair use)

16 See, e.g., <u>Marcus v. Rowley</u>, 695 F. 2d 1171 (9th Cir. 1983) (public school teacher sued for use of copyrighted material in her home economics class failed to prove that her copying was within the bounds of fair use)

17 The section includes the "employee or agent of a nonprofit educational institution, library or archives acting within the scope of his or her employment."

18 17 U.S.C. Section 504

19 17 U.S.C. Section 511

20 17 U.S.C. Section 110(1)

21 H.Rep. No. 94-1476 (1976) at

22 H.Rep. 94-1476, 94th Cong., 2d Sess., 85-86 (1976) Under certain conditions, however, the performance may be classified as a nonprofit performance and be exempted under that provision.

23 To transmit a performance or display is to communicate it by any device or process whereby images or sounds are received beyond the place from which they are sent. 17 U.S.C. '101

24 H.R. 2281, Public Law 105-304, 112 Stat. 2827. Several education organizations, including NSBA, lobbied Congress for language that would specifically note that fair use applied to the digital media. Their attempts were unsuccessful.

25 The National Information Infrastructure Task Force, created by then-President Clinton, under the direction of the Department of Commerce, established the Working Group on Intellectual Property. It was this Working Group that convened the Conference on Fair Use to develop guidelines for the fair use of digital technology.

26 The Consortium of College and University Media Centers (CCUMC) presented the Multimedia Guidelines to CONFU.

27 It should be noted that while the multimedia guidelines were drafted with the participation of the National School Boards Association, NSBA specifically declined to endorse these guidelines.

28 In addition to NSBA, the American Association of School Administrators, American Association of State Colleges and Universities, American Council on Education, National Association of Elementary School Principals, National Association of Secondary School Principals, and the National Education Association have opposed the Multimedia Guidelines.

29 17 U.S.C. '117 excludes from infringement the copying of computer programs for archival purposes as well as the copying that is necessary in order to adapt the program for specific uses or hardware.

30 A sample permission letter is included in the Appendix.

31 NSBA maintains a policy network, with sample policies from member school districts. Many state school boards associations offer a similar service.

Appendix 1

How Technology Can Affect Ethical Behavior

Schools play a major role in reinforcing traditional societal values and helping students see how those values apply to the use of information technology... Schools can take action on technology ethics on two fronts: setting school policy that provides a model for students to follow, and incorporating technology ethics issues into the curriculum.

While many of our traditional values can be stretched to fit the new environment of information technology, ...some aspects of this new environment can make that fit difficult to perceive. A child who would never think of searching through a classmate's desk to read her personal diary might feel free to access and read the same classmate's diary stored in a word processing file on a computer network. A teenager who would never dream of robbing a bank might experience fewer qualms about attempting to steal funds from the bank electronically. Why?

One explanation is that the technology removes us from the concrete object: the book, the actual money. Another explanation is that, by using the computer to commit an unethical or criminal act, the perpetrator often believes that he or she can escape detection. As the fear of being caught decreases, so does the student's need to engage in soul-searching.

Information technology also introduces psychological distance to the scenario.... When we interact with others face-to-face and behave unethically, we experience first-hand the harm we have caused and perhaps ostracism or even quick rebuttal—and the resulting feelings can reinforce our ethical norms. When we use information technology in a way that does harm to others, the act feels less personal because we cannot see or hear the other person in the exchange.... For instance, if a group of students gains unauthorized access to a corporate computer network, they might feel pleased that they have succeeded in "beating the system" but might never realize the disruption they have caused to the employees who run and use the network. The fact that information technology makes it easier to target victims we don't know and who don't know us, adds to the feeling of anonymity and distance.

Source: Excerpted from Jay P. Sivin & Ellen R. Bialo, "How Technology Can Affect Ethical Behavior," *Ethical Use of Information Technologies in Education: Important Issues for America's Schools* (Washington, DC: U. S. Department of Justice, Office of Justice Programs, National Institute of Justice, April 1992). Available online: http://www.eff.org/Intellectual_property/ethical_use_of_info_tech_in_education.paper

Appendix 2

School Law & Technology Hypotheticals

The following hypotheticals are based on actual, documented situations and occurrences. Each hypothetical relates to one or more issues discussed in Chapter 1, "Student Learning and the Law of School Technology."

LIABILITY

1. Who's responsible when a student uses school computers for live chats and is victimized by an online "friend" whom she met during her school-time access?

Sandra is a 13-year-old middle school pupil who spends hours on the Internet at school. She has no Internet access at home, and her parents know very little about the Internet. One of her favorite pastimes is to enter electronic chat rooms and talk to others about personal things like relationships, love, and life. Her teacher lets her use the Internet in the classroom every day at lunch because she has no friends. Sandra meets a wonderful 13-year-old boy on the Internet. He is everything that she dreamed a boy should be. She arranges to meet him at a local fast food hamburger restaurant. It turns out her online friend is actually a 45-year-old child molester. Sandra is abducted and molested. Sandra and her parents sue the school for negligent supervision.

Could the district and teacher be held liable?

Answer:

The school district and the teacher could be held liable if a jury concluded that the teacher's supervision was not reasonable under the circumstances. A competent plaintiff's attorney would be able to make strong arguments that supervision was inadequate by using school administrators from other districts to discuss the inherent risks of questionable encounters on the Web and the necessity to supervise student use of the Web. This hypothetical is based on a situation that occurred in San Diego. (See generally *Dailey v. Los Angeles Unified School Dist.*, 2 Cal.3d 741, 470 P.2d 360 (1970). Sets forth duty of student supervision by school personnel.)

Policy Solution:

The hold harmless and release language in the school's student Internet use agreement (see Chapter 1) would be useful in arguing that the school district and teacher cannot be held liable because such liability was waived. (*Cf. Aaris v. Las Virgenes Unified School Dist.*, 64 Cal.App.4th 1112 (Cal. 1998) upholding release language with a school)

2. Why Johnny can build bombs

Johnny is a very smart and inquisitive seventh grader who has no Internet access at home. His teacher has just taught him how to use the Internet to find information about different subjects that Johnny might want to know about—for instance, the gross national products of South American countries, the yearly rainfall in the Congo, etc., all of which are topics Johnny is supposed to be studying in geography class. Johnny is more interested in other things and spends hours on the Internet learning how to make letter bombs and pipe bombs. No one seemed to notice what Johnny was up to until he blew up the local convenience store across the street from the school. The store owner sues the school, and Johnny's parents demand copies of all e-mail Johnny has sent using the school's e-mail account.

Is the school liable, and is there any problem with turning over the e-mail?

Answer:

Again, if a jury felt that supervision was inadequate, the school district would be liable. The school's student Internet use agreement does not create a waiver of liability for third parties—which in this case is the store owner. With regard to releasing Johnny's e-mail messages, students have rights to privacy covered by the Electronic Communications Privacy Act. (18 U.S.C. § 2510 et seq.) Thus, it would be unlawful to intercept Johnny's e-mail without his permission.

Policy Solution:

Policies will not control liability to third parties such as the convenience store owner. But in agreeing to the school's student Internet use agreement, Johnny would have waived certain privacy rights, including giving the school permission to monitor his e-mail.

3. Student images—Where does privacy begin?

A student named Tim takes pictures of the Roosevelt High School cheerleaders and school leaders to advertise fun graduation trips for seniors—trips like Beer Blast to Cancun, Maui Invasion, Moonlight in Bermuda (without your parents), etc. The cheerleaders and school leaders did not give permission for their pictures to be used in advertising on the Internet. One enterprising cheerleader, being short of money for college, sues the school district for invasion of her privacy for using her picture for commercial purposes without her permission.

Can the school district be held liable for anything?

Answer:

The student's privacy rights have been violated by commercially appropriating her image to advertise without her permission. The school could be liable to her. (Restatement (Second) of Torts, § 652C (1965))

Policy Solution:

Control access to district-related Web sites, and require consent to post student pictures and names on such Web sites.

FREE EXPRESSION

4. Freedom of expression

Roosevelt High has an open guest book for people to share what they think of the school programs and Web site. The school district invites community participation on its Web site with chat rooms, guest books, and bulletin boards. The school board has proclaimed that they want the school district's Web site to be as open for expression as a school board meeting. Members welcome input on their Web site about curriculum, important political issues related to education, and anything that the community considers important with regard to education.

Sophomore Joe Hearst prints an underground newspaper and distributes it at school. He enjoys criticizing various things about the school, using four-letter words, and publishing questionable stories and poetry that include vulgar language. Since all of this is done privately by Joe, he actually has a legal right to engage in such activity on campus.

No one pays attention to Joe anymore. He therefore posts his newsletter on the district Web site bulletin board. To make sure people pay attention, he now writes shameful articles about which teachers are drunks and have driving under the influence (DUI) charges now or in the past. He makes allegations about which teachers cheat on their spouses and with whom and when, and which teachers have made inappropriate advances to students. Joe's articles are widely read and have popularized the district Web site considerably. Joe is even dreaming of a career with one of the Hollywood gossip tabloids.

Can the district keep Joe's material off its Web site?

Answer:

Under First Amendment freedom of expression law, when a school opens a forum (like the Web site in this scenario) to unrestricted public expression, it has difficulty thereafter controlling the content or who has access to that forum. Roosevelt High has opened its Web site to the community to discuss its schools. Joe can argue that he is discussing the community schools by revealing which teachers are fit examples for youth. With an open forum Web site, a court would probably allow Joe to continue his underground link to the school's Web site. (See generally *Board of Westside Community Schools v. Mergens, 109 S.Ct. 3240 (1990)* and *Planned Parenthood of Southern Nevada, Inc. v. Clark County School Dist.*, 941 F.2d 817 (1991). Both cases discuss the issue of school forums.)

Policy Solutions:

The school could eliminate expression such as Joe's in two main ways. It could prevent the Web site forum from being used in certain ways and discontinue its use as a community forum for discussion on education issues. The district could also adopt a school district-related Web site policy that designates the site as a "closed forum," for district use only, to transmit information to the public.

5. Political speech

Local activist Bull Loney is running for the school board. He connects his Web site to the Roosevelt Web site to engage in political debate about the school board election. Many consider his statements to be reactionary and racist. He decries the shameful new religion of secular humanism being taught in our schools and make scurrilous remarks about the abilities of various school employees.

Now what?

Answer:

If the Web site provides an open forum for expression, it's the cyber-age equivalent of a soap box in a park. Therefore, even the most objectionable individuals can have their say.

Policy Solution:

The school could eliminate expression such as Bull's in three ways. (1) It could close the Web site forum to certain uses and discontinue its use as a community forum for discussion on education issues. (2) It could adopt a school district-related Web site policy that designates the site as a "closed forum," for district use only, to transmit information to the public. (3) The district could create a service mark for the school name so that anyone using the school's name as an identifier (such as the name of a link or in the Web page name itself) could be required to seek permission from the district or cease using the school name in identifying a site or link.

6. Religion and prayer in cyberspace—How are schools linked?

The Roosevelt High School Mergens club (Christian prayer club) begins posting material on the school Web site too. Contrary to what one might expect, it is one of the most visited connections—not because of its religious content, but because of it's "Sinner of the Week" column. Club members vote on which teacher or student was the biggest sinner during the previous week, write about which commandment was broken, and give details on the actions that the sinner took in breaking the commandment.

Would the district have a problem prohibiting this column?

Answer:

Again, an open forum creates the opportunity for anyone to post material on the Web site. Since schools must be neutral toward religion, they may not restrict their own Mergens prayer club from posting information on the Web site. (See *Westside Community Schools v. Mergens*, 109 S.Ct. 3240 (1990))

CENSORSHIP

7. Filters—The good news and the bad

Roosevelt High School deploys an Internet filter to censor access to inappropriate Web sites, including those featuring sexually explicit or hate content. The civil liberties group objects to censorship in any form and threatens litigation. The organization demands that the filter be removed immediately and cites, as authority for their position, cases in which public libraries have been forced to remove filters.

Can the filter be legally retained?

Answer:

The filter can be lawful though the manner in which it is implemented could cause problems. Schools may censor materials going into their libraries and classrooms if there are legitimate pedagogical concerns to support such censorship. (*Board of Education, Island Trees Union Free District # 26 v. Pico*, 457 U.S. 853 (1982) and *McCarthy v. Fletcher*, 254 Cal.Rptr. 714 (1989).) Similarly, schools should be able to censor inappropriate Internet material. If the filter is indiscriminate and filters out harmless material, or if the filter is used to screen information based on political content of Web sites, there could be problems with its implementation.

Policy Solution:

Administrative regulations and policies related to Internet filters should provide a rationale for using filters. The best solution for staving off legal problems in this area is to designate responsible persons to oversee the filtering process and direct those responsible to employ sound educational criteria to determine what is filtered.

CYBER-NUISANCES

8. Dealing with sexually explicit pranks

Traditionally, Benson High students each year "tipped" the Rough Rider statue at Roosevelt High before the big game between the two schools. Since students were caught and punished over the last few years, this year's crop of Benson students have become more creative. They logged onto the Roosevelt home page, clicked onto the "Rough Rider Guest book," and instead of posting comments about the school and the Web page, they posted several dozen sexually explicit pictures.

Can they be punished? Can the pictures be removed?

Answers:

Given proper due process, the students could be punished. The Webmaster can remove the pictures; however, if the Webmaster is a student and off-campus when school officials discover the pictures (as was the situation in the actual case upon which this hypothetical is based), immediate removal of the pictures could be problematic.

Policy Solution:

Make sure the district's Web site policy designates district personnel as supervisors over district-related Web sites. The policy should, in general, also eliminate chat rooms and guest books. However, guest books could be used if they are moderated by an adult Webmaster who is the only person able to post or authorize posting of material on the Web site.

9. Squelching school disparagement

A group of enterprising students at John F. Kennedy High create their own Web site without using any school district technology. They use a private server for their site, "Kennedy High Hi-Times." On the site, the students write articles favoring the legalization of illicit drugs and euthanasia of teachers over the age of 30, as well as articles disparaging the school and its administration, faculty, and student leaders. It is possible that users visiting the site consider it to be sponsored by the school.

Does the school have any leverage in preventing publication of this Web site and its content?

Answer:

These students are not violating any district policy by publishing a Web site on their own Web server without using any district technology.

Policy Solutions:

If the district has established a service mark (similar to trademark) for the school's name, the district may lawfully require the students to remove the name "Roosevelt High" from the Web site name.

Appendix 3

Annotated Policy on
EMPLOYEE COMPUTER AND INTERNET USE – CODE: GCSA

Annotations by
Bruce W. Smith, Esq.
Drummond Woodsum & MacMahon
June 2001

This is an annotated version of a sample policy on employee computer use. The annotations are included to explain some of the policy provisions and to assist those drafting policies in considering the options they have. All annotations are set out in shaded boxes and are not intended to be part of the policy (suggested policy language is given in roman type.) This sample should be used as a reference only, and any policy should be reviewed by legal counsel before adoption.[1]

A note on acceptable use policies in general: The introduction of Internet-connected computers into schools for student and staff use has spawned a virtual epidemic of policy-writing. Many of these policies are extremely long and complex. School boards should adopt policies that they believe will best meet the needs of their schools, students and staff. This writer has a bias toward simpler, user-friendly policies that can be read and understood by the people for whom they are written. While the more elaborate policies may sometimes provide more specific guidance, they are often written defensively, to protect schools from liabilities that are often only remotely likely to arise. A policy that is couched in legalese and full of disclaimers—the legal masterpiece—may be more likely to gather dust on a shelf than to actually be used by the people to whom it is addressed.

The **[name of school unit]** provides computers, networks and Internet access to support the educational mission of the schools and to enhance the curriculum and learning opportunities for students and school staff.

A statement of the purpose for which the school offers computer technology and communications helps to establish the reasonableness of the use rules that follow. The statement of purpose may be quite simple, as it is in this policy, although further elaboration is possible.

Local boards should decide whether employee use of computers will be limited to job-related duties or whether some level of personal use will be allowed. The following paragraphs illustrate two different approaches that local school units may want to consider:

Employees may utilize the school unit's computers, networks and Internet services only for purposes related to the schools and the performance of their jobs, and no personal use of any kind is permitted.

This approach limits computer and network use to work-related purposes only. The advantage of this approach is that it establishes a very clear line between permissible and non-permissible uses. There will be no ambiguity about whether personal uses are permitted, and there will be no doubt that the school unit will not have created a limited public forum under the First Amendment. Many school districts, however, do not wish to forbid all personal use, and some believe that allowing personal use will help teachers to learn the technology more quickly.

OR

Employees are to utilize the school unit's computers, networks and Internet services for school-related purposes and performance of job duties. Incidental personal use of school computers is permitted as long as such use does not interfere with the employee's job duties and performance, with system operations or other system users. "Incidental personal use" is defined as use by an individual employee for occasional personal communications. Employees are reminded that such personal use must comply with this policy and all other applicable policies, procedures and rules.

This approach allows personal use, but seeks to close the door on any uses of technology that are not personal to the individual employee. See the rules below for the types of activity that might be prohibited. At times, it may be difficult to distinguish reasonably between "incidental personal use" and other non-permitted uses. In addition, an employee might claim that even allowing such limited personal use creates a limited public forum under the First Amendment, and that restrictions of communications based on their content would violate the First Amendment. To date, we are not aware of any court rulings addressing the question of whether a school's computer network may in any circumstances be regarded as a limited public forum affording employees free speech rights. In the case of *Urofsky v. Gilmore*, 216 F.3d 401 (4th Cir. 2000), the Fourth Circuit Court of Appeals held that a Virginia law barring state employees from accessing sexually explicit web sites on state computers did not violate the free speech rights or the "academic freedom" of university professors. The court reasoned that the state employees did not have any enforceable First Amendment rights while using state computers or performing their duties. This decision supports the authority of schools to restrict employee access to content on the Internet.

Any employee who violates this policy and/or any rules governing use of the school unit's computers will be subject to disciplinary action, up to and including discharge. Illegal uses of the school unit's computers will also result in referral to law enforcement authorities.

It is important to put employees on notice that the rules are mandatory and that violations may result in discipline. More specific delineation of disciplinary consequences is not necessary.

All **[name of school unit]** computers remain under the control, custody and supervision of the school unit. The school unit reserves the right to monitor all computer and Internet activity by employees. Employees have no expectation of privacy in their use of school computers.

As employees of governmental entities, school staff members have a right under the Fourth Amendment of the U.S. Constitution to be free of unreasonable searches and seizures. In *O'Connor v. Ortega*, 480 U.S. 709 (1987) the Supreme Court ruled that the Fourth Amendment applies only when the public employee has "an expectation of privacy that society is prepared to consider reasonable." Whether such an expectation exists depends upon the circumstances, including the employer's policies and practices. If the employee has a reasonable expectation of privacy, the public employer may conduct a work search only if it is "reasonable under all the circumstances." The federal Electronic Communications Privacy Act (ECPA), Pub.L.No. 99-508, 100 Stat. 1848, also protects the privacy of electronic communications, including electronic mail. The employees' expectations regarding privacy, or the lack of it, are largely determined by the employer's policies, rules and practices concerning use of the school computer system. By clearly stating that employees retain no expectation of privacy in school computers, data and communications, the school will retain the right to monitor and search employee computers.

Each employee authorized to access the school unit's computers, networks and Internet services is required to sign an acknowledgment form (GCSA-E) stating that they have read this policy and the accompanying rules. The acknowledgment form will be retained in the employee's personnel file.

Many schools require employees to sign computer use agreements in which they agree to comply with all school policies and rules. This approach gives rise to two questions: (1) Are such agreements really necessary? (2) Does the proffering of such agreements create more problems than it prevents? Taking the second question first, we have found that employees sometimes balk at signing agreements on computer use. Rarely if ever are employees required to sign agreements to follow other school policies and rules, so this is a deviation from normal practice. With regard to the first question, employees are expected to follow school board policies and rules. As long as they are notified of the policy, there is no reason why it cannot be enforced whether the employee has signed an agreement or not. The purpose of the acknowledgment contained in this policy is to ensure that all employees do receive notice of the policy. If the school has an effective means of distributing the policy to all staff members (e.g., include a copy in the pay envelope), a signed acknowledgment is not needed.

The superintendent shall be responsible for overseeing the implementation of this policy and the accompanying rules, and for advising the board of the need for any future amendments or revisions to the policy/rules. The superintendent may develop additional administrative procedures/rules governing the day-to-day management and operations of the school unit's computer system as long as they are consistent with the board's policy/rules. The superintendent may delegate specific responsibilities to building principals and others as he/she deems appropriate.

The approach taken in this policy is to have the board adopt a brief, general policy addressing only the major issues and to authorize the superintendent to develop and to amend as necessary more specific rules. School boards wishing to review and include all rules in their policy may certainly do so. It is important to bear in mind that acceptable use policies will need frequent revision and updating as experience and changes in technology develop.

Adopted: _____

Endnote

[1] This annotated policy was written by Bruce W. Smith and has been adopted by the Maine School Management Association as their model policy.

Appendix 4

Annotated Policy on
EMPLOYEE COMPUTER AND INTERNET USE RULES – CODE: GCSA-R

Annotations by
Bruce W. Smith, Esq.
Drummond Woodsum & MacMahon

The organizational structure, computer systems and resources of local school units vary widely. These sample rules are intended to provide general guidance for local boards in developing rules that meet local needs and conditions. The board should involve school staff with expertise in this area in developing the rules. MSMA also recommends that local boards have the rules reviewed by their legal counsel prior to adoption All annotations are shaded and are not intended to be part of the policy. Sample policy language is given in Roman type.[1]

The intent of these board-level rules is to provide employees with general requirements for utilizing the school unit's computers, networks and Internet services. The board rules may be supplemented by more specific administrative procedures and rules governing day-to-day management and operation of the computer system.

These rules provide general guidelines and examples of prohibited uses for illustrative purposes, but do not attempt to state all required or prohibited activities by users. Employees who have questions regarding whether a particular activity or use is acceptable should seek further guidance from the system administrator **[or insert other appropriate administrator]**.

Try as you might, you will never adopt rules that will anticipate every possible situation. Perhaps it should go without saying, but it is still a good idea to let employees know that these rules are not necessarily comprehensive and that they should use good judgment at all times.

Failure to comply with board policy GCSA (Employee Computer and Internet Use), these rules and/or other established procedures or rules governing computer use may result in disciplinary action, up to and including discharge. Illegal uses of the school unit's computers will also result in referral to law enforcement authorities.

A. Access to School Computers, Networks and Internet Services
The level of access that employees have to school unit computers, networks and Internet services is based upon specific employee job requirements and needs.

B. Acceptable Use
Employee access to the school unit's computers, networks and Internet services is provided for administrative, educational, communication and research purposes consistent with the school unit's educational mission, curriculum and instructional goals. General rules and expectations for professional behavior and communication apply to use of the school unit's computers, networks and Internet services.

NOTE: As discussed in the note in policy GCSA, local boards should decide whether employee use of computers will be limited to job-related duties or whether some level of personal use will be allowed. The following paragraphs illustrate two different approaches that local school units may want to consider. *The same language used in policy GCSA should be repeated here.*

Employees may utilize the school unit's computers, networks and Internet services only for purposes related to the schools and the performance of their jobs, and no personal use of any kind is permitted.

OR

Employees are to utilize the school unit's computers, networks and Internet services for school-related purposes and performance of job duties. Incidental personal use of school computers is permitted as long as such use does not interfere with the employee's job duties and performance, with system operations or other system users. "Incidental personal use" is defined as use by an individual employee for occasional personal communications. Employees are reminded that such personal use must comply with this policy and all other applicable policies, procedures and rules.

The alternatives above are identical to those in the board policy. See the notes contained in the board policy.

C. Prohibited Use

The employee is responsible for his/her actions and activities involving school unit computers, networks and Internet services, and for his/her computer files, passwords and accounts. General examples of unacceptable uses which are expressly prohibited include, but are not limited to, the following:

The following list is fairly extensive, but it is probably not possible to anticipate all inappropriate uses.

1. Any use that is illegal or in violation of other board policies, including harassing, discriminatory or threatening communications and behavior; violations of copyright laws, etc.;

These rules deal largely with the use of computers as tools of communication. The same rules that govern communications in other contexts in schools should apply to computer use. It is not necessary to list these other rules and policies in detail. The above statement makes it clear that policies concerning sexual and other forms of discriminatory (racial, disability, etc.) harassment apply to computer communications. Copyright laws also apply to materials downloaded and reproduced and to materials posted on the Internet just as they do to books and periodicals used by teachers. Teachers should have some basic training in copyright law to prevent inadvertent violations, whether in digital media or more traditional media.

2. Any use involving materials that are obscene, pornographic, sexually explicit or sexually suggestive;

3. Any inappropriate communications with students or minors;

A federal law enacted in December of 2000 now requires all schools receiving E-rate discounts or federal Title III funds for Internet connections have filtering or blocking technology for all users to block obscenity and child pornography. A more detailed discussion of the law is contained in chapter 1. It has been argued by some that this restriction could violate employees' First Amendment rights. One federal court has addressed a challenge to a Virginia state law which prohibited university professors, as well as other state employees, from accessing sexually explicit materials on state computers. In the case of *Urofsky v. Gilmore*, 216 F.3d 401 (4th Cir. 2000), the United States Courts of Appeals for the Fourth Circuit ruled that the law did not violate the First Amendment. Courts generally permit greater restrictions on speech in K-12 schools than in public universities, so we are confident that this provision is lawful.

4. Any use for private financial gain, or commercial, advertising or solicitation purposes;

5. Any use as a forum for communicating by e-mail or any other medium with other school users or outside parties to solicit, proselytize, advocate or communicate the views of an individual or non-school sponsored organization; to solicit membership in or support of any non-school sponsored organization; or to raise funds for any non-school sponsored purpose, whether profit or non-for-profit. No employee shall knowingly provide school e-mail addresses to outside parties whose intent is to communicate with school employees, students and/or their families for non-school purposes. Employees who are uncertain as to whether particular activities are acceptable should seek further guidance from the building principal or other appropriate administrator.

This rule places extensive restrictions on employee use of school computers and networks for non-school related communications. Due to first amendment concerns, it is important that such restrictions be "content-neutral," that is, that they treat all viewpoints equally. For example, it is questionable whether the school could ban all religious views but allow the expression of political or social views, or whether the school could allow solicitation for the Boy Scouts but not the Republican Party. It is better, legally, to ban all solicitation and organizational activities than to do so on a piecemeal basis. Without a rule such as this one, a school's computer network may become a limited public forum where users gain some First Amendment protection. Two reasons why the school may wish to avoid creating a public forum are: (1) that use for non-school purposes increases traffic on computers and servers and distracts employees from their work; (2) once a forum is created, the authority of the school to prevent certain speech that might be thought of as inappropriate will be limited.

Restriction of the content of employee communications is a sensitive area of policy making. Policy drafters should consult the school's attorney concerning any revisions to the above rule.

6. Any communication that represents personal views as those of the school unit or that could be misinterpreted as such;

Courts have generally recognized the authority of schools to prevent employees or students from presenting their own views in such a manner that they could be attributed to the school.

7. Downloading or loading software or applications without permission from the system administrator;

> The purpose of this rule is to prevent filling school computer hard drives with unrelated material, to prevent the degradation of school systems by introduction of software that could interfere with the operation of school software, and to prevent employees from making extensive personal use of school computers.

8. Opening or forwarding any e-mail attachments (executable files) from unknown sources and/or that may contain viruses;

> This rule will protect school users from internally-generated junk e-mail (Internet jokes, urban legends, etc.), and the school system from non-school related e-mail traffic.

9. Sending mass e-mails to school users or outside parties for school or non-school purposes without the permission of the system administrator [**or other designated administrator**].

10. Any malicious use or disruption of the school unit's computers, networks and Internet services or breach of security features;

11. Any misuse or damage to the school unit's computer equipment;

12. Misuse of the computer passwords or accounts (employee or other users);

13. Any communications that are in violation of generally accepted rules of network etiquette and/or professional conduct;

14. Any attempt to access unauthorized sites;

15. Failing to report a known breach of computer security to the system administrator;

16. Using school computers, networks and Internet services after such access has been denied or revoked; and

17. Any attempt to delete, erase or otherwise conceal any information stored on a school computer that violates these rules.

> The purpose of this rule is to make it clear that it is against the rules to try to hide evidence of misconduct.

D. No Expectation of Privacy

The school unit retains control, custody and supervision of all computers, networks and Internet services owned or leased by the school unit. The school unit reserves the right to monitor all computer and Internet activity by employees and other system users. Employees have no expectation of privacy in their use of school computers, including e-mail messages and stored files.

As public employees, school employees have some privacy protection under the Fourth Amendment to the United States Constitution. In *O'Connor v. Ortega*, 480 U.S. 709 (1987), the Supreme Court ruled that the Fourth Amendment applies only when the public employee has "an expectation of privacy that society is prepared to consider reasonable." Whether such an expectation exists depends upon the circumstances, including the employer's policies and practices. If the employee has a reasonable expectation of privacy, the public employer may conduct a work search only if it is "reasonable under all the circumstances" (Id. at 725). By stating clearly that employees should have no expectation of privacy in anything stored on school computers and that the school retains the right to access them at any time for any reason, schools should be able to avoid any legal claims based on an employee's privacy rights.

E. Confidentiality of Information

Employees are expected to use appropriate judgment and caution in communications concerning students and staff to ensure that personally identifiable information remains confidential.

Student information is made confidential by the Family Educational Rights and Privacy Act (FERPA). School staff members may communicate confidential student information to other staff members only for legitimate educational purposes. E-mail may be used for this purpose, with due regard for the need to maintain confidentiality.

F. Staff Responsibilities to Students

Teachers, staff members and volunteers who utilize school computers for instructional purposes with students have a duty of care to supervise such use. Teachers, staff members and volunteers are expected to be familiar with the school unit's policies and rules concerning student computer and Internet use and to enforce them. When, in the course of their duties, employees/volunteers become aware of student violations, they are expected to stop the activity and inform the building principal [**or other appropriate administrator**].

The most important means to prevent student misuse of school computers is supervision. This section is intended to affirm the duty of staff members to supervise student use and to report any student violations.

G. Compensation for Losses, Costs and/or Damages

The employee shall be responsible for any losses, costs or damages incurred by the school unit related to violations of policy GCSA and/or these rules.

H. School Unit Assumes No Responsibility for Unauthorized Charges, Costs, or Illegal Use

The school unit assumes no responsibility for any unauthorized charges made by employees, including but not limited to credit card charges, subscriptions, long distance telephone charges, equipment and line costs, or for any illegal use of its computers such as copyright violations.

I. Employee Acknowledgment Required

Each employee authorized to access the school unit's computers, networks and Internet services is required to sign an acknowledgment form (GCSA-E) stating that they have read policy GCSA and these rules. The acknowledgment form will be retained in the employee's personnel file.

Some schools have required employees to sign agreements indicating that they will comply with computer use rules, and in some districts, employees have balked at signing such agreements. Employees are not ordinarily required to execute written agreements that they will comply with other rules and policies, and we do not think a written agreement is necessary with regard to this policy. The form that follows is simply an acknowledgment, designed to ensure that all employees receive notice of the policy and the rules. The acknowledgment can be used to provide evidence that an employee was aware of the rules should a violation occur.

Adopted: _____

Endnote

1   This annotated policy was written by Bruce W. Smith and has been adopted by the Maine School Management Association as their model policy.

EMPLOYEE COMPUTER/INTERNET USE ACKNOWLEDGMENT FORM (CODE: GCSA-A)

No employee shall be allowed to use school computers or the Internet until he/she has signed and returned this acknowledgment.

I have read policy GCSA – Employee Computer and Internet Use and GCSA-R – Employee Computer and Internet Use Rules and understand their terms and conditions.

_____   _____

Signature   Date

Appendix 5

Conference on Fair Use (CONFU) Guidelines

The National Information Infrastructure Task Force, created in 1993 by then-President Clinton, under the direction of the Department of Commerce, established the Working Group on Intellectual Property. It was this Working Group that convened the Conference on Fair Use (CONFU) in 1994 to develop guidelines for the fair use of digital technology. In May 1998, the final CONFU report was issued (http://www2.uspto.gov/web/offices/dcom/olia/confu/).

CONFU produced four sets of proposed guidelines, two of which are included in this appendix: *Fair Use Guidelines for Educational Multimedia* and *Proposal for Educational Fair Use Guidelines for Distance Learning*.

CONFU guidelines are **NOT** law. They are offered as a resource for educators considering digital copyright issues.

FAIR USE GUIDELINES FOR EDUCATIONAL MULTIMEDIA[1]
TABLE OF CONTENTS

1. INTRODUCTION

1.1 Preamble

Fair use is a legal principle that provides certain limitations on the exclusive rights[2] of copyright holders. The purpose of these guidelines is to provide guidance on the application of fair use principles by educators, scholars and students who develop multimedia projects using portions of copyrighted works under fair use rather than by seeking authorization for non-commercial educational uses. These guidelines apply only to fair use in the context of copyright and to no other rights.

There is no simple test to determine what is fair use. Section 107 of the Copyright Act[3] sets forth the four fair use factors which should be considered in each instance, based on particular facts of a given case, to determine whether a use is a "fair use": (1) the purpose and character of use, including whether such use is of a commercial nature or is for nonprofit educational purposes, (2) the nature of the copyrighted work, (3) the amount and substantiality of the portion used in relation to the copyrighted work as a whole, and (4) the effect of the use upon the potential market for or value of the copyrighted work.

While only the courts can authoritatively determine whether a particular use is fair use, these guidelines represent the participants'[4] consensus of conditions under which fair use should generally apply and examples of when permission is required. Uses that exceed these guidelines may or may not be fair use. The participants also agree that the more one exceeds these guidelines, the greater the risk that fair use does not apply.

The limitations and conditions set forth in these guidelines do not apply to works in the public domain — such as US Government works or works on which copyright has expired for which there are no copyright restrictions — or to works for which the individual or institution has obtained permission for the particular use. Also, license agreements may govern the uses of some works and users should refer to the applicable license terms for guidance.

The participants who developed these guidelines met for an extended period of time and the result represents their collective understanding in this complex area. Because digital technology is in a dynamic phase, there may come a time when it is necessary to review the guidelines. Nothing in these guidelines shall be construed to apply to the fair use privilege in any context outside of educational and scholarly uses of educational multimedia projects.

This Preamble is an integral part of these guidelines and should be included whenever the guidelines are reprinted or adopted by organizations and educational institutions. Users are encouraged to reproduce and distribute these guidelines freely without permission; no copyright protection of these guidelines is claimed by any person or entity.

1.2 Background

These guidelines clarify the application of fair use of copyrighted works as teaching methods are adapted to new learning environments. Educators have traditionally brought copyrighted books, videos, slides, sound recordings and other media into the classroom, along with accompanying projection and playback equipment. Multimedia creators integrated these individual instructional resources with their own original works in a meaningful way, providing compact educational tools that allow great flexibility in teaching and learning. Material is stored so that it may be retrieved in a nonlinear fashion, depending on the needs or interests of learners. Educators can use multimedia projects to respond spontaneously to students' questions by referring quickly to relevant portions. In addition, students can use multimedia projects to pursue independent study according to their needs or at a pace appropriate to their capabilities. Educators and students want guidance about the application of fair use principles when creating their own multimedia projects to meet specific instructional objectives.

1.3 Applicability of These Guidelines

(Certain basic terms used throughout these guidelines are identified in bold and defined in this section.)

These guidelines apply to the use, without permission, of portions of lawfully acquired copyrighted works in educational multimedia projects which are created by educators or students as part of a systematic learning activity by nonprofit educational institutions. Educational multimedia projects created under these guidelines incorporate students' or educators' original material, such as course notes or commentary, together with various copyrighted media formats including but not limited to, motion media, music, text material, graphics, illustrations, photographs and digital software which are combined into an integrated presentation. Educational institutions are defined as nonprofit organizations whose primary focus is supporting research and instructional activities of

educators and students for noncommercial purposes. For the purposes of these guidelines, educators include faculty, teachers, instructors and others who engage in scholarly research and instructional activities for educational institutions. The copyrighted works used under these guidelines are lawfully acquired if obtained by the institution or individual through lawful means such as purchase, gift or license agreement

but not pirated copies. Educational multimedia projects which incorporate portions of copyrighted works under these guidelines may be used only for educational purposes in systematic learning activities including use in connection with non-commercial curriculum-based learning and teaching activities by educators to students enrolled in courses at nonprofit educational institutions or otherwise permitted under Section 3. While these guidelines refer to the creation and use of educational multimedia projects, readers are advised that in some instances other fair use guidelines such as those for off-air taping may be relevant.

2. PREPARATION OF EDUCATIONAL MULTIMEDIA PROJECTS USING PORTIONS OF COPYRIGHTED WORKS

These uses are subject to the Portion Limitations listed in Section 4. They should include proper attribution and citation as defined in Sections 6.2.

2.1 By Students:

Students may incorporate portions of lawfully acquired copyrighted works when producing their own educational multimedia projects for a specific course.

2.2 By Educators for Curriculum-Based Instruction:

Educators may incorporate portions of lawfully acquired copyrighted works when producing their own educational multimedia projects for their own teaching tools in support of curriculum-based instructional activities at educational institutions.

3. PERMITTED USES OF EDUCATIONAL MULTIMEDIA PROJECTS CREATED UNDER THESE GUIDELINES

Uses of educational multimedia projects created under these guidelines are subject to the Time, Portion, Copying and Distribution Limitations listed in Section 4.

3.1 Student Use:

Students may perform and display their own educational multimedia projects created under Section 2 of these guidelines for educational uses in the course for which they were created and may use them in their own portfolios as examples of their academic work for later personal uses such as job and graduate school interviews.

3.2 Educator Use for Curriculum-Based Instruction:

Educators may perform and display their own educational multimedia projects created under Section 2 for curriculum-based instruction to students in the following situations:

3.2.1 for face-to-face instruction,

3.2.2 assigned to students for directed self-study,

3.2.3 for remote instruction to students enrolled in curriculum-based courses and located at remote sites, provided over the educational institution's secure electronic network in real-time, or for after class review or directed self-study, provided there are technological limitations on access to the network and educational multimedia project (such as a password or PIN) and provided further that the technology prevents the making of copies of copyrighted material.

If the educational institution's network or technology used to access the educational multimedia project created under Section 2 of these guidelines cannot prevent duplication of copyrighted material, students or educators may use the multimedia educational projects over an otherwise secure network for a period of only 15 days after its initial real-time remote use in the course of instruction or 15 days after its assignment for directed self-study. After that period, one of the two use copies of the educational multimedia project may be placed on reserve in a learning resource center, library or similar facility for on-site use by students enrolled in the course. Students shall be advised that they are not permitted to make their own copies of the educational multimedia project.

3.3 Educator Use for Peer Conferences:

Educators may perform or display their own educational multimedia projects created under Section 2 of these guidelines in presentations to their peers, for example, at workshops and conferences.

3.4 Educator Use for Professional Portfolio

Educators may retain educational multimedia projects created under Section 2 of these guidelines in their personal portfolios for later personal uses such as tenure review or job interviews.

4. LIMITATIONS - TIME, PORTION, COPYING AND DISTRIBUTION

The preparation of educational multimedia projects incorporating copyrighted works under Section 2, and the use of such projects under Section 3, are subject to the limitations noted below.

4.1 Time Limitations

Educators may use their educational multimedia projects created for educational purposes under Section 2 of these guidelines for teaching courses, for a period of up to two years after the first instructional use with a class. Use beyond that time period, even for educational purposes, requires permission for each copyrighted portion incorporated in the production. Students may use their educational multimedia projects as noted in Section 3.1.

4.2 Portion Limitations

Portion limitations mean the amount of a copyrighted work that can reasonably be used in educational multimedia projects under these guidelines regardless of the original medium from which the copyrighted works are taken. In the aggregate means the total amount of copyrighted material from a single copyrighted work that is permitted to be used in an educational multimedia project without permission under these guidelines. These limitations apply cumulatively to each educator's or student's multimedia project(s) for the same academic semester, cycle or term. All students should be instructed about the reasons for copyright protection and the need to follow these guidelines. It is understood, however, that students in kindergarten through grade six may not be able to adhere rigidly to the portion limitations in this section in theirnindependent development of educational multimedia projects. In any event, each such project retained under Sections 3.1 and 4.3 should comply with the portion limitations in this section.

4.2.1 Motion Media

Up to 10% or 3 minutes, whichever is less, in the aggregate of a copyrighted motion media work may be reproduced or otherwise incorporated as part of an educational multimedia project created under Section 2 of these guidelines.

4.2.2 Text Material

Up to 10% or 1000 words, whichever is less, in the aggregate of a copyrighted work consisting of text material may be reproduced or otherwise incorporated as part of an educational multimedia project created under Section 2 of these guidelines. An entire poem of less than 250 words may be used, but no more than three poems by one poet, or five poems by different poets from any anthology may be used. For poems of greater length, 250 words may be used but no more than three excerpts by a poet, or five excerpts by different poets from a single anthology may be used.

4.2.3 Music, Lyrics, and Music Video

Up to 10%, but in no event more than 30 seconds, of the music and lyrics from an individual musical work (or in the aggregate of extracts from an individual work), whether the musical work is embodied in copies or audio or audiovisual works, may be reproduced or otherwise incorporated as a part of a multimedia project created under Section 2. Any alterations to a musical work shall not change the basic melody or the fundamental character of the work.

4.2.4 Illustrations and Photographs

The reproduction or incorporation of photographs and illustrations is more difficult to define with regard to fair use because fair use usually precludes the use of an entire

work. Under these guidelines a photograph or illustration may be used in its entirety but no more than 5 images by an artist or photographer may be reproduced or otherwise incorporated as part of an educational multimedia project created under Section 2. When using photographs and illustrations from a published collective work, not more than 10% or 15 images, whichever is less, may be reproduced or otherwise incorporated as part of an educational multimedia project created under Section 2.

4.2.5 Numerical Data Sets

Up to 10% or 2500 fields or cell entries, whichever is less, from a copyrighted database or data table may be reproduced or otherwise incorporated as part of an educational multimedia project created under Section 2 of these guidelines. A field entry is defined as a specific item of information, such as a name or Social Security number, in a record of a database file. A cell entry is defined as the intersection where a row and a column meet on a spreadsheet.

4.3 Copying and Distribution Limitations

Only a limited number of copies, including the original, may be made of an educator's educational multimedia project. For all of the uses permitted by Section 3, there may be no more that two use copies only one of which may be placed on reserve as described in Section 3.2.3.

An additional copy may be made for preservation purposes but may only be used or copied to replace a use copy that has been lost, stolen, or damaged. In the case of a jointly created educational multimedia project, each principal creator may retain one copy but only for the purposes described in Sections 3.3 and 3.4 for educators and in Section 3.1 for students.

5. EXAMPLES OF WHEN PERMISSION IS REQUIRED

5.1 Using Multimedia Projects for Non-Educational or Commercial Purposes
Educators and students must seek individual permissions (licenses)before using copyrighted works in educational multimedia projects for commercial reproduction and distribution.

5.2 Duplication of Multimedia Projects Beyond Limitations Listed in These Guidelines

Even for educational uses, educators and students must seek individual permissions for all copyrighted works incorporated in their personally created educational multimedia projects before replicating or distributing beyond the limitations listed in Section 4.3.

5.3 Distribution of Multimedia Projects Beyond Limitations Listed in These Guidelines

Educators and students may not use their personally created educational multimedia projects over electronic networks, except for uses as described in Section 3.2.3, without obtaining permissions for all copyrighted works incorporated in the program.

6. IMPORTANT REMINDERS

6.1 Caution in Downloading Material from the Internet

Educators and students are advised to exercise caution in using digital material downloaded from the Internet in producing their own educational multimedia projects, because there is a mix of works protected by copyright and works in the public domain on the network. Access to works on the Internet does not automatically mean that these can be reproduced and reused without permission or royalty payment and, furthermore, some copyrighted works may have been posted to the Internet without authorization of the copyright holder.

6.2 Attribution and Acknowledgment

Educators and students are reminded to credit the sources and display the copyright notice 8 and copyright ownership information if this is shown in the original source, for all works incorporated as part of educational multimedia projects prepared by educators and students, including those prepared under fair use. Crediting the source must adequately identify the source of the work, giving a full bibliographic description where available (including author, title, publisher, and place and date of publication). The copyright ownership information includes the copyright notice (8, year of first publication and name of the copyright holder).

The credit and copyright notice information may be combined and shown in a separate section of the educational multimedia project (e.g. credit section) except for images incorporated into the project for the uses described in Section 3.2.3. In such cases, the copyright notice and the name of the creator of the image must be incorporated into the image when, and to the extent, such information is reasonably available; credit and copyright notice information is considered "incorporated" if it is attached to the image file and appears on the screen when the image is viewed. In those cases when displaying source credits and copyright ownership information on the screen with the image would be mutually exclusive with an instructional objective (e.g. during examinations in which the source credits and/or copyright information would be relevant to the examination questions),those images may be displayed without such information being simultaneously displayed on the screen. In such cases, this information should be linked to the image in a manner compatible with such instructional objectives.

6.3 Notice of Use Restrictions

Educators and students are advised that they must include on the opening screen of their multimedia project and any accompanying print material a notice that certain materials are included under the fair use exemption of the U.S. Copyright Law and have been prepared according to the educational multimedia fair use guidelines and are restricted from further use.

6.4 Future Uses Beyond Fair Use

Educators and students are advised to note that if there is a possibility that their own educational multimedia project incorporating copyrighted works under fair use could later result in broader dissemination, whether or not as commercial product, it is strongly recommended that they take steps to obtain permissions during the development process for all copyrighted portions rather than waiting until after completion of the project.

6.5 Integrity of Copyrighted Works: Alterations

Educators and students may make alterations in the portions of the copyrighted works

they incorporate as part of an educational multimedia project only if the alterations support specific instructional objectives. Educators and students are advised to note that alterations have been made.

6.6 Reproduction or Decompilation of Copyrighted Computer Programs

Educators and students should be aware that reproduction or decompilation of copyrighted computer programs and portions thereof, for example the transfer of underlying code or control mechanisms, even for educational uses, are outside the scope of these guidelines.

6.7 Licenses and Contracts

Educators and students should determine whether specific copyrighted works, or other data or information are subject to a license or contract. Fair use and these guidelines shall not preempt or supersede licenses and contractual obligations

---

1   These Guidelines shall not be read to supersede other preexisting education fair use guidelines that deal with the Copyright Act of 1976.

2   See Section 106 of the Copyright Act.

3   The Copyright Act of 1976, as amended, is codified at 17 U.S.C. Sec.101 et seq.

4   The names of the various organizations participating in this dialog appear at the end of these guidelines and clearly indicate the variety of interest groups involved, both from the standpoint of the users of copyrighted material and also from the standpoint of copyright owners.

APPENDIX A

(Endorsements and letters of support received as of September 19, 1996)

1. ORGANIZATIONS ENDORSING THESE GUIDELINES:

Agency for Instructional Technology (AIT)
American Association of Community Colleges (AACC)
American Society of Journalists and Authors (ASJA)
American Society of Media Photographers, Inc. (ASMP)
American Society of Composers, Authors and Publishers (ASCAP)
Association for Educational Communications and Technology (AECT)
Association for Information Media and Equipment (AIME)
Association of American Publishers (AAP)
Association of American Colleges and Universities (AAC&U)
Association of American University Presses, Inc. (AAUP)
Broadcast Music, Inc. (BMI)
Consortium of College and University Media Centers (CCUMC)
Instructional Telecommunications Council (ITC)
Maricopa Community Colleges/Phoenix
Motion Picture Association of America (MPAA)

Music Publishers' Association of the United States (MPA)
Software Publishers Association (SPA)

2. INDIVIDUAL COMPANIES AND INSTITUTIONS ENDORSING THESE GUIDELINES:

Houghton Mifflin
McGraw-Hill
Time Warner, Inc.

3. U.S. GOVERNMENTAL AGENCIES SUPPORTING THESE GUIDELINES:

U.S. National Endowment for the Arts (NEA)
U.S. Copyright Office

APPENDIX B
ORGANIZATIONS PARTICIPATING IN GUIDELINE DEVELOPMENT:

Being a participant does not necessarily mean the organization has or will endorse these guidelines.
Agency for Instructional Technology (AIT)
American Association of Community Colleges (AACC)
American Association for Higher Education (AAHE)
American Library Association (ALA)
American Society of Journalists and Authors (ASJA)
American Society of Media Photographers (ASMP)
Artists Rights Foundation
Association of American Colleges and Universities (AAC&U)
Association of American Publishers (AAP)
-Harvard University Press
-Houghton Mifflin
-McGraw-Hill
-Simon and Schuster
-Worth Publishers
Association of College and Research Libraries (ACRL)
Association for Educational Communications and Technology (AECT)
Association for Information Media and Equipment (AIME)
Association of Research Libraries (ARL)
Authors Guild, Inc.
Broadcast Music, Inc. (BMI)
Consortium of College and University Media Centers (CCUMC)
Copyright Clearance Center (CCC)
Creative Incentive Coalition (CIC)
Directors Guild of America (DGA)
European American Music Distributors Corp.
Educational institutions participating in guideline discussion
-American University
-Carnegie Mellon University
-City College/City University of New York
-Kent State University
-Maricopa Community Colleges/Phoenix

-The Pennsylvania State University
-University of Delaware
Information Industry Association (IIA)
Instructional Telecommunications Council (ITC)
International Association of Scientific, Technical and Medical Publishers
Motion Picture Association of America (MPAA)
Music Publishers Association (MPA)
National Association of State Universities and Land-Grant Colleges(NASULGC)
National Council of Teachers of Mathematics (NCTM)
National Educational Association (NEA)
National Music Publishers Association (NMPA)
National School Boards Association (NSBA)
National Science Teachers Association (NSTA)
National Video Resources (NVR)
Public Broadcasting System (PBS)
Recording Industry Association of America (RIAA)
Software Publishers Association (SPA)
Time Warner, Inc.
U.S. Copyright Office
U.S. National Endowment for the Arts (NEA)
Viacom, Inc.

Prepared by the Educational Multimedia Fair Use Guidelines
Development Committee, July 17, 1996.

**PROPOSAL FOR EDUCATIONAL FAIR USE
GUIDELINES FOR DISTANCE LEARNING**[1]
Performance & Display of Audiovisual and Other Copyrighted Works

1.1 PREAMBLE

Fair use is a legal principle that provides certain limitations on the exclusive rights[2] of copyright holders. The purpose of these guidelines is to provide guidance on the application of fair use principles by educational institutions, educators, scholars and students who wish to use copyrighted works for distance education under fair use rather than by seeking authorization from the copyright owners for non-commercial purposes. The guidelines apply to fair use only in the context of copyright.

There is no simple test to determine what is fair use. Section 107 of the Copyright Act[3] sets forth the four fair use factors which should be considered in each instance, based on the particular facts of a given case, to determine whether a use is a "fair use": (1) the purpose and character of the use, including whether use is of a commercial nature or is for nonprofit educational purposes, (2) the nature of the copyrighted work, (3) the amount and substantiality of the portion used in relation to the copyrighted work as a whole, and (4) the effect of the use upon the potential market for or value of the copyrighted work.

While only the courts can authoritatively determine whether a particular use is a fair use, these guidelines represent the endorsers' consensus of conditions under which fair use should generally apply and examples of when permission is required. Uses that exceed these guidelines may or may not be fair use. The endorsers also agree that the more one exceeds these guidelines, the greater the risk that fair use does not apply.

The limitations and conditions set forth in these guidelines do not apply to works in the public domain — such as U.S. government works or works on which the copyright has expired for which there are no copyright restrictions — or to works for which the individual or institution has obtained permission for the particular use. Also, license agreements may govern the uses of some works and users should refer to the applicable license terms for guidance.

The participants who developed these guidelines met for an extended period of time and the result represents their collective understanding in this complex area. Because digital technology is in a dynamic phase, there may come a time when it is necessary to revise these guidelines. Nothing in these guidelines should be construed to apply to the fair use privilege in any context outside of educational and scholarly uses of distance education. The guidelines do not cover non-educational or commercial digitization or use at any time, even by nonprofit educational institutions. The guidelines are not intended to cover fair use of copyrighted works in other educational contexts such as educational multimedia projects,4 electronic reserves or digital images which may be addressed in other fair use guidelines.

This Preamble is an integral part of these guidelines and should be included whenever the guidelines are reprinted or adopted by organizations and educational institutions. Users are encouraged to reproduce and distribute these guidelines freely without permission; no copyright protection of these guidelines is claimed by any person or entity.

1.2 BACKGROUND

Section 106 of the Copyright Act defines the right to perform or display a work as an exclusive right of the copyright holder. The Act also provides, however, some exceptions under which it is not necessary to ask the copyright holder's permission to perform or display a work. One is the fair use exception contained in Section 107, which is summarized in the preamble. Another set of exceptions, contained in Sections 110(1)-(2), permit instructors and students to perform or display copyrighted materials without permission from the copyright holder under certain carefully defined conditions.

Section 110(1) permits teachers and students in a nonprofit educational institution to perform or display any copyrighted work in the course of face-to-face teaching activities. In face-to-face instruction, such teachers and students may act out a play, read aloud a poem, display a cartoon or a slide, or play a videotape so long as the copy of the videotape was lawfully obtained. In essence, Section 110(1) permits performance and display of any kind of copyrighted work, and even a complete work, as a part of face-to-face instruction. Section 110(2) permits performance of a nondramatic literary or musical work or display of any work as a part of a transmission in some distance learning contexts, under the specific conditions set out in that Section. Section 110(2) does not permit performance of dramatic or audiovisual works as a part of a transmission The statute further requires that the transmission be directly related and of material assistance to the teaching content of the transmission and that the transmission be received in a classroom or other place normally devoted to instruction or by persons whose disabilities or special circumstances prevent attendance at a classroom or other place normally devoted to instruction.

The purpose of these guidelines is to provide guidance for the performance and display of copyrighted works in some of the distance learning environments that have developed since the enactment of Section 110 and that may not meet the specific conditions of Section 110(2). They permit instructors who meet the conditions of these guidelines to perform and display copyrighted works as if they were engaged in face-to-face instruction. They may, for example, perform an audiovisual work, even a complete one, in a one-time transmission to students so long as they meet the other conditions of these guidelines. They may not, however, allow such transmissions to result in copies for students unless they have permission to do so, any more than face-to-face instructors may make copies of audiovisual works for their students without permission.

The developers of these guidelines agree that these guidelines reflect the principles of fair use in combination with the specific provisions of Sections 110(1)-(2). In most respects, they expand the provisions of Section 110(2). In some cases, students and teachers in distance learning situations may want to perform and display only small portions of copyrighted works that may be permissible under the fair use doctrine even in the absence of these guidelines. Given the specific limitations set out in Section 110(2), however, the participants believe that there may be a higher burden of demonstrating that fair use under Section 107 permits performance or display of more than a small portion of a copyrighted work under circumstances not specifically authorized by Section 110(2).

1.3 DISTANCE LEARNING IN GENERAL

Broadly viewed, distance learning is an educational process that occurs when instruction is delivered to students physically remote from the location or campus of program origin, the main campus, or the primary resources that support instruction. In this process, the requirements for a course or program may be completed through remote communications with instructional and support staff including either one-way or two-way written, electronic or other media forms.

Distance education involves teaching through the use of telecommunications technologies to transmit and receive various materials through voice, video and data. These avenues of teaching often constitute instruction on a closed system limited to students who are pursuing educational opportunities as part of a systematic teaching activity or curriculum and are officially enrolled in the course. Examples of such analog and digital technologies include telecourses, audio and video teleconferences, closed broadcast and cable television systems, microwave and ITFS, compressed and full-motion video, fiber optic networks, audiographic systems, interactive videodisk, satellite-based and computer networks.

2. APPLICABILITY AND ELIGIBILITY

2.1 APPLICABILITY OF THE GUIDELINES

These guidelines apply to the performance of lawfully acquired copyrighted works not included under Section 110(2) (such as a dramatic work or an audiovisual work) as well as to uses not covered for works that are included in Section 110(2). The covered uses are (1) live interactive distance learning classes (i.e., a teacher in a live class with all or some of the students at remote locations) and (2) faculty instruction recorded without students present for later transmission. They apply to delivery via satellite, closed circuit television or a secure computer network. They do not permit circumventing anti-copying mechanisms embedded in copyrighted works.

These guidelines do not cover asynchronous delivery of distance learning over a computer network, even one that is secure and capable of limiting access to students enrolled in the course through PIN or other identification system. Although the participants believe fair use of copyrighted works applies in some aspects of such instruction, they did not develop fair use guidelines to cover these situations because the area is so unsettled. The technology is rapidly developing, educational institutions are just beginning to experiment with these courses, and publishers and other creators of copyrighted works are in the early stages of developing materials and experimenting with marketing strategies for computer network delivery of distance learning materials. Thus, consideration of whether fair use guidelines are needed for asynchronous computer network delivery of distance learning courses perhaps should be revisited in three to five years.

In some cases, the guidelines do not apply to specific materials because no permission is required, either because the material to be performed or displayed is in the public domain, or because the instructor or the institution controls all relevant copyrights. In other cases, the guidelines do not apply because the copyrighted material is already subject to a specific agreement. For example, if the material was obtained pursuant to a license, the terms of the license apply. If the institution has received permission to use copyrighted material specifically for distance learning, the terms of that permission apply.

2.2 ELIGIBILITY

2.2.1 ELIGIBLE EDUCATIONAL INSTITUTION: These guidelines apply to nonprofit educational institutions at all levels of instruction whose primary focus is supporting research and instructional activities of educators and students but only to their nonprofit activities. They also apply to government agencies that offer instruction to their employees.

2.2.2 ELIGIBLE STUDENTS: Only students officially enrolled for the course at an eligible institution may view the transmission that contains works covered by these guidelines. This may include students enrolled in the course who are currently matriculated at another eligible institution. These guidelines are also applicable to government agency employees who take the course or program offered by the agency as a part of their official duties.

3. WORKS PERFORMED FOR INSTRUCTION

3.1 RELATION TO INSTRUCTION: Works performed must be integrated into the course, must be part of systematic instruction and must be directly related and of material assistance to the teaching content of the transmission. The performance may not be for entertainment purposes.

4. TRANSMISSION AND RECEPTION

4.1 TRANSMISSION (DELIVERY): Transmission must be over a secure system with technological limitations on access to the class or program such as a PIN number, password, smartcard or other means of identification of the eligible student.

4.2 RECEPTION: Reception must be in a classroom or other similar place normally devoted to instruction or any other site where the reception can be controlled by the eligible institution. In all such locations, the institution must utilize technological means to prevent copying of the portion of the class session that contains performance of the copyrighted work.

5. LIMITATIONS:

5.1 ONE TIME USE: Performance of an entire copyrighted work or a large portion thereof may be transmitted only once for a distance learning course. For subsequent performances, displays or access, permission must be obtained.

5.2 REPRODUCTION AND ACCESS TO COPIES

5.2.1 RECEIVING INSTITUTION: The institution receiving the transmission may record or copy classes that include the performance of an entire copyrighted work, or a large portion thereof, and retain the recording or copy for up to 15 consecutive class days (i.e., days in which the institution is open for regular instruction) for viewing by students enrolled in the course. Access to the recording or copy for such viewing must be in a controlled environment such as a classroom, library or media center, and the institution must prevent copying by students of the portion of the class session that contains the performance of the copyrighted work. If the institution wants to retain the recording or copy of the transmission for a longer period of time, it must obtain permission from the rightsholder or delete the portion which contains the performance of the copyrighted work.

5.2.2 TRANSMITTING INSTITUTION: The transmitting institution may, under the same terms, reproduce and provide access to copies of the transmission containing the performance of a copyrighted work; in addition, it can exercise reproduction rights provided in Section 112(b).

6. MULTIMEDIA

6.1 COMMERCIALLY PRODUCED MULTIMEDIA: If the copyrighted multimedia work was obtained pursuant to a license agreement, the terms of the license apply. If, however, there is no license, the performance of the copyrighted elements of the multimedia works may be transmitted in accordance with the provisions of these guidelines.

7. EXAMPLES OF WHEN PERMISSION IS REQUIRED:

7.1 Commercial uses: Any commercial use including the situation where a nonprofit educational institution is conducting courses for a for-profit corporation for a fee such as supervisory training courses or safety training for the corporation's employees.

7.2. Dissemination of recorded courses: An institution offering instruction via distance learning under these guidelines wants to further disseminate the recordings of the course or portions that contain performance of a copyrighted work.

7.3 Uncontrolled access to classes: An institution (agency) wants to offer a course or program that contains the performance of copyrighted works to non-employees.

7.4 Use beyond the 15-day limitation: An institution wishes to retain the recorded or copied class session that contains the performance of a copyrighted work not covered in Section 110(2). (It also could delete the portion of the recorded class session that contains the performance).

---

1   See Exec. Order No. 12864, 3 C.F.R. 634 (1993).

2   Information Infrastructure Task Force, National Telecommunications and Information Administration, National Information Infrastructure: Agenda for Action (1993).

3   Information Infrastructure Task Force, Global Information Infrastructure: Agenda for Cooperation (1995).

4   For list of participating agencies, see Information Infrastructure Task Force, Working Group on Intellectual Property Rights, Intellectual Property and the National Information Infrastructure: The Report of the Working Group on Intellectual Property Rights (1995) (hereinafter WHITE PAPER) at App. 3.

APPENDIX A: ORGANIZATIONS ENDORSING THESE GUIDELINES
[To be added after endorsements are received.]

APPENDIX B: ORGANIZATIONS PARTICIPATING IN GUIDELINE DEVELOPMENT
[Being a participant does not necessarily mean that the organization has or will endorse these guidelines.]

American Association of Community Colleges
American Association of Law Libraries
American Council of Learned Societies
Association of American Publishers
Association of American Universities
Association of College and Research Libraries
Association of Research Libraries
Broadcast Music, Inc.
Consortium of College and University Media Centers
Creative Incentive Coalition
Houghton Mifflin
Indiana Partnership for Statewide Education
John Wiley & Sons, Inc.
Kent State University
National Association of State Universities and Land Grant Colleges
National Geographic Society
National School Board Association
Special Libraries Association
State University of New York
U.S. Copyright Office
University of Texas System
Viacom, Inc.

Appendix 6

Sample Letter
Request for Permission to Use Print Material

Date

Permissions Department* [Call and ascertain proper name and title.]

Publisher

Re: Permission to Use Copyrighted Materials

Dear Sir/Madam:

Kindly consider this letter as a request to use the following copyrighted materials:

[Describe material—including title, page numbers, publication date. If possible, include a copy of the material.]

These materials will be used for:

[Describe when, where, and how the material will be used. Include, where appropriate, number of copies; duration; name of class, instructor, & institution; name of publication & issue.]

Should you have a specific copyright notice, please specify it here:

A duplicate copy of this letter has been enclosed for your convenience. Kindly return a signed copy to my attention. Enclosed is a self-addressed, stamped envelope in which to enclose the signed form.

If you are not the copyright holder, kindly inform me to whom I must address my request.

Sincerely,

School Administrator, or Classroom Teacher

Permission Granted:

Name (please print) _____

Signed _____

Title _____

Date _____

*Assumes material in question has been published and that the publisher owns the copyright.

Appendix 7

Guidelines for Educational Uses of Music

In a joint letter dated April 30,1976, representatives of the Music Publishers Association of the United States, Inc., the National Music Publishers Association, Inc., the Music Teachers National Association, the Music Educators National Conference, the National Association of Schools of Music, and the Ad Hoc Committee on Copyright Law Revision, wrote to Chairman Kastenmeier as follows:

> During the hearings on H.R. 2223 in June 1975, you and several of your subcommittee members suggested that concerned groups should work together in developing guidelines which would be helpful to clarify Section 107 of the bill.
>
> Representatives of music educators and music publishers delayed their meetings until guidelines had been developed relative to books and periodicals. Shortly after that work was completed and those guidelines were forwarded to your subcommittee, representatives of the undersigned music organizations met together with representatives of the Ad Hoc Committee on Copyright Law Revision to draft guidelines relative to music.
>
> We are very pleased to inform you that the discussions thus have been fruitful on the guidelines which have been developed. Since private music teachers are an important factor in music education, due consideration has been given to the concerns of that group.
>
> We trust that this will be helpful in the report on the bill to clarify Fair Use as it applies to music.

The following guidelines were developed and approved in April 1976 by the Music Publishers' Association of the United States, Inc., the National Music Publishers' Association, Inc., the Music Teachers National Association, the Music Educators National Conference, the National Association of Schools of Music, and the Ad Hoc Committee on Copyright Law Revision.

Guidelines for Educational Uses of Music

The purpose of the following guidelines is to state the minimum and not the maximum standards of educational fair use under Section 107 of HR 2223. The parties agree that the conditions determining the extent of permissible copying for educational purposes may change in the future; that certain types of copying permitted under these guidelines may not be permissible in the future, and conversely that in the future other types of copying not permitted under these guidelines may be permissible under revised guidelines.

Moreover, the following statement of guidelines is not intended to limit the types of copying permitted under the standards of fair use under judicial decision and which are stated in Section 107 of the Copyright Revision Bill. There may be instances in which copying which does not fall within the guidelines stated below may nonetheless be permitted under the criteria of fair use.

A. Permissible Uses

1. Emergency copying to replace purchased copies which for any reason are not available for an imminent performance provided purchased replacement copies shall be substituted in due course.

2. For academic purposes other than performance, single or multiple copies of excerpts of works may be made, provided that the excerpts do not comprise a part of the whole which would constitute a performable unit such as a section, movement or aria, but in no case more than 10 percent of the whole work. The number of copies shall not exceed one copy per pupil.

3. Printed copies which have been purchased may be edited or simplified provided that the fundamental character of the work is not distorted or the lyrics, if any, altered or lyrics added if none exist.

4. A single copy of recordings of performances by students may be made or evaluation or rehearsal purposes and may be retained by the educational institution or individual teacher.

5. A single copy of a sound recording (such as a tape, disc, or cassette) of copyrighted music may be made from sound recordings owned by an educational institution or an individual teacher for the purpose of constructing aural exercises or examinations and may be retained by the educational institution or individual teacher. (This pertains only to the copyright of the music itself and not to any copyright which may exist in the sound recording.)

B. Prohibitions

1. Copying to create or replace or substitute for anthologies, compilations or collective works.

2. Copying of or from works intended to be "consumable" in the course of study or of teaching such as workbooks, exercises, standardized tests and answer sheets and like material.

3. Copying for the purpose of performance, except as in A(1) above.

4. Copying for the purpose of substituting for the purchase of music, except as in A(1) and A(2) above.

5. Copying without inclusion of the copyright notice which appears on the printed copy.

Source: *Reproduction of Copyrighted Works by Educators and Librarians.* Circular 21. 1995. Washington, DC: Library of Congress, Copyright Office. Available online: http://www.purduenc.edu/cd/copyright/broadcast.htm.

Appendix 8

Guidelines for Off-Air Recordings of Broadcast Programming for Educational Purposes

In March 1979, Congressman Robert Kastenmeier, chairman of the House Subcommittee on Courts, Civil Liberties, and Administration of Justice, appointed a Negotiating Committee consisting of representatives of education organizations, copyright proprietors, and creative guilds and unions. The following guidelines reflect the Negotiating Committee's consensus as to the application of "fair use" to the recording, retention, and use of television broadcast programs for educational purposes. They specify periods of retention and use of such off-air recordings in classrooms and similar places devoted to instruction and for homebound instruction. The purpose of establishing these guidelines is to provide standards for both owners and users of copyrighted television programs.

1. The guidelines were developed to apply only to off-air recording by nonprofit educational institutions.

2. A broadcast program may be recorded off-air simultaneously with broadcast transmission (including simultaneous cable retransmission) and retained by a nonprofit educational institution for a period not to exceed the first forty-five (45) consecutive calendar days after date of recording. Upon conclusion of such retention period, all off-air recordings must be erased or destroyed immediately. "Broadcast programs" are television programs transmitted by television stations for reception by the general public without charge.

3. Off-air recordings may be used once by individual teachers in the course of relevant teaching activities, and repeated once only when instructional reinforcement is necessary, in classrooms and similar places devoted to instruction within a single building, cluster or campus, as well as in the homes of students receiving formalized home instruction, during the first ten (10) consecutive school days in the forty-five (45) day calendar day retention period. "School days" are school session days — not counting weekends, holidays, vacations, examination periods, and other scheduled interruptions — within the forty-five (45) calendar day retention period.

4. Off-air recordings may be made only at the request of and used by individual teachers, and may not be regularly recorded in anticipation of requests. No broadcast program may be recorded off-air more than once at the request of the same teacher, regardless of the number of times the program may be broadcasted.

5. A limited number of copies may be reproduced from each off-air recording to meet the legitimate needs of teachers under these guidelines. Each such additional copy shall be subject to all provisions governing the original recording.

Source: Excerpted from the House Report on piracy and counterfeiting amendments (H.R. 97-495, pages 8-9). *Reproduction of Copyrighted Works by Educators and Librarians.* Circular 21. 1995. Washington, DC: Library of Congress, Copyright Office. Available online: http://www.purduenc.edu/cd/copyright/broadcast.htm.

Glossary of Technology Terms

Application Service Provider (ASP) — A service firm that delivers, manages, and remotely hosts software applications through centrally located servers. Usually done under a rental or lease arrangement.

ASCII – American Standard Code for Information Interchange. A set of alphanumeric and special control characters. ASCII files are also known as plain text files.

BPS – Bits per second. A measurement of the volume of data that a modem is capable of transmitting. Currently, a typical modem speed is 56Kbps (56,000 bits per second).

Bookmark – A pointer to a particular Web site. Within browsers, a user can bookmark interesting pages and then return to them easily.

Browser, browsing – A program run on a computer that allows one to view World Wide Web pages. Examples include Netscape, Microsoft's Internet Explorer and Mosaic.

Chat room – An online location where participants can exchange notes, converse and share data live as they type messages to one another.

Downloading – The electronic transfer of information from one computer to another, generally from a larger computer to a smaller one, such as from a server to a personal computer.

Electronic bulletin board – A shared file where users can enter information for other users to read or download. Many bulletin boards are set up according to general topics and are accessible throughout a network.

E-mail – Electronic mail is comprised of messages delivered via computer networks to individuals' online "mailboxes." One can send not only messages, but also files, artwork, sound and video. E-mail is used both as a noun and as a verb (i.e., I received her e-mail two days after I e-mailed her.)

E-mail group – An electronic mailing list used to share information about a topic of common interest. When a person subscribes to an e-mail group, he or she receives – and in many cases can send – e-mail messages for all participants to read. Participants usually subscribe via a central service, and lists often have a moderator who manages the information flow and content. Listserv®, a commercial product marketed by L-Soft International Inc., and Majordomo, which is *freeware*, are popular mailing list servers. The term "listserv" often is used incorrectly to refer to any mailing list server.

E-zines – Electronic magazines distributed over the Internet — sometimes called zines (pronouced "zeens").

FAQ – Frequently asked questions. A collection of common questions and answers on a particular subject.

Flame – An insulting message, perhaps even malicious, exchanged via e-mail or within newsgroups. A series of flames are known as flame wars. Sometimes a flaming missive is intentionally sent in such huge quantities that it becomes a burden to the recipient.

FreeWare – Software that is copyrighted but freely available for downloading and use. Compare with *shareware*.

GIF – Graphics interchange format. A common image format. Most images seen on Web pages are GIF files.

Home page – The main page of a Web site, usually where the site's items are listed for easy access. Also, the Web site that automatically loads each time the user launches a *browser*.

HTML – HyperText Markup Language. Used to author documents on the Web.

HTTP – HyperText Transfer Protocol. The Web's protocol that defines formatting and transmission of messages and how browsers and Web servers respond to commands.

Hyperlink – A connection between pieces of information within one document or two separate documents, possibly at different Web sites. Clicking with a mouse on one will take the user to the linked location.

Hypertext – A database system that allows text, graphics, sounds and other "objects" to be linked to each other – such as at a Web site or in a CD-ROM program.

Intellectual Property – A general reference to the legal rights granted to authors, artists, inventors and other creators to control the use and dissemination of their original ideas or unique way of expressing those ideas. Applies with equal force to the Internet and other technologies.

Internet – The Internet is a global network of millions of computers that provides access to a wide range of information housed on different Web sites and enables fast, inexpensive communication among people.

Intranet vs. Internet – Internet documents and information are available to anyone in the world, except for items protected by security systems. Intranet documents and information are available only to computers within a specific network. Intranets are closed and secure; the Internet is open. Both intranets and Internet are based on *TCP/IP* protocols.

ISDN – Integrated services digital network. An international communications standard for high-speed transmission of voice, video and data over digital telephone lines.

ISP – Internet service provider. A company that provides a connection to the Internet via either a *dial-up connection or a direct connection.*

IP address – Internet protocol address. Every computer on the Internet has a unique identifying number, such as 111.0.11.0. IP addresses are assigned by the Inter NIC Registration Service *(http://www.internic.net).*

JPEG – Joint Photographic Experts Group, a common image format. Most of the images embedded into Web pages are GIFs, but sometimes, especially in art or photographic Web sites, one can click on the image to bring up a higher resolution JPEG version of the same image.

Link – Another name for a hyperlink. It is the place in a Web document where the viewer can click to travel or link to a different Web location. Links collectively make a web of information.

Listserv® – See *e-mail group* above.

MIDI – Musical instrument digital interface, a standard the music industry has adopted for controlling electronic musical devices, such as synthesizers.

Modem – A device for transmitting electronic signals between computers (which store information digitally) and analog telephone lines. The term is derived from "modulator-demodulator," describing what a modem does to signals. A cable modem operates over cable television lines.

MPEG – Motion Picture Experts Group. An industry group and the video compression standards and file formats they develop to produce excellent quality in relatively small files. Video files found on the Internet are commonly stored in the MPEG format. Also, full-length movies housed on CD are usually stored in the MPEG format.

Multimedia – A combination of media types such as graphics, animation, audio and/or video in a single document.

Newsgroup – An online discussion group covering a shared interest of participants. A "newsreader" program, such as those available at some Web browser sites, is required to view and post messages to the group. Unlike with an *e-mail group*, access is not limited to a list of individuals.

Search Engines – Search engines enable computer users to research a topic, in an organized and methodical way, on the Internet. Examples of common search engines are AltaVista *(http://www.altavista.com)* and Lycos (http://www.lycos.com).

Server – A computer or other device that manages a network's resources. See *Web server.*

Shareware – Microcomputer software, distributed through public domain channels, for which the author requests compensation from those who use it.

Spam – A slang term for e-mail that is the electronic equivalent of junk mail. Usually advertisements, jokes, or notices of no real value to the recipient.

T-1 LINE – A high speed, high-bandwidth telephone connection. It carries 1.544 megabits per second of data and is capable of handling tens of thousands of requests for information daily. Businesses often connect to the Internet using T-1 lines.

TCP/IP – Transmission Control Protocol/Internet Protocol is a combined set of protocols that perform the transfer of data between two computers. TCP monitors and ensures correct transfer of data. IP receives the data from TCP, breaks it up into "packets," and ships it off to a network within the Internet. TCP/IP is also used as a name for a protocol that incorporates these functions and others.

URL – Uniform Resource Locator. A standardized resource address system used on the Web. The URL describes everything that is necessary for a Web browser to locate a resource. It defines the name of the computer, the site it is housed on, the path, and the file name.

Webmaster – An individual who manages a Web site, possibly charged with site design and maintenance, response to queries and monitoring use.

Web server – The host computer that houses a home page and Web site. It allows full time access to the site.

Web site – The combination of a home page and any additional Web pages that represent a school district, individual, organization or business in the Internet community. It can offer text documents, graphics, video, audio and interactive forms.

World Wide Web – The Web, a system of Internet servers supporting documents formatted in *HTML* so that elements – such as text, graphics, audio and video items – can be linked when users click a mouse on designated spots at Web sites. Web browsers are used to access the World Wide Web.

Publications of the National School Boards Association's Council of School Attorneys

Contracting with Architects: A School District's Perspective (February 1991) This monograph is intended to assist school attorneys and school administrators involved in school construction projects with selecting an architect; understanding the relationship between the architect and school district; and contract negotiation. Also included is an analysis of the 1987 AIA owner-architect agreement (B-141) and suggested amendments to the general conditions of the contract for construction (A-201). Please note that this publication is limited to the 1987 standard forms. 50 pages. ISBN 0-88364-159-3. (List $25, National Affiliates and Council Members $20.)

Desk Reference on Significant U.S. Supreme Court Cases Affecting Public Schools (*Revised Edition* 2000) This desk reference provides attorneys and laymen alike with quick access to the name, citation and/or rule of virtually every U.S. Supreme Court case in which a public school district was a party and a substantive decision was rendered (however, it does not analyze the decision). It includes an extensive word index, table of cases with full parallel citations and table of constitutional and statutory provisions. 118 pages. ISBN 0-88364-227-1 (List $25, National Affiliates and Council members $20).

Legal Guidelines for Curbing School Violence (March 1995) This publication covers such issues as search and seizure, metal detectors, students' due process rights, discipline of students with disabilities, tort and constitutional liability, hate speech, dress codes and gangs, keeping weapons out of schools and working with the criminal justice system. 162 pages. ISBN 0-88364-195-X (List $30, National Affiliates and Council Members $25).

Legal Handbook on School Athletics (March 1997) Topics on this issue include discipline of athletes: due process considerations, eligibility rules protecting high school athletes, participation of private school and disabled students, drug testing, Title IX, public school sports and religion, injuries during physical education classes and extracurricular activities, spectator issues, student athletics and insurance issues, athletic personnel and volunteer issues. 120 pages. ISBN 0-88364-206-9 (List $35, National Affiliates and Council Members $28).

Religion & Public Schools: Striking A Constitutional Balance (August 2001) This publication discusses the latest developments in the law, including the Supreme Court's decisions in *Milford*, *Mitchell*, *Santa Fe* and *Agostini*. This monograph focuses on the effect of the Establishment and Free Exercise Clauses of the First Amendment on public schools. It analyzes the constitutional issues surrounding accommodating employee religious beliefs, wearing of religious garb, curriculum content, school prayer/moment of silence, holiday observances, equal access, home schools and much more. 240 pages. ISBN 0-88364-244-1 (List $35, National Affiliates and Council members $28).

Safe Schools, Safe Communities (September 2000). This publication examines how schools and communities can work together to make our schools safe. Among the topics discussed are the need to balance school safety needs and the rights of individual students, how to deal with threats of violence, the role of the school attorney in response to violence, and how to work with the media in times of crisis. 98 pages. ISBN 0-88364-238-7 (List $25, National Affiliates and Council Members $20).

School Board Member Liability Under Section 1983 (April 1992) This publication seeks to explain clearly and accurately in layman's terms the basics of civil rights law under Section 1983. It focuses on the types of claims most commonly brought under Section 1983 against school boards and presents factual circumstances and how the courts have applied the law in immunity defenses. 44 pages. ISBN 0-88364-134-8 (List $15, National Affiliates and Council members $12).

2000 Advocacy Seminar Notebook. This loose-leaf trial notebook is a compilation of the presentations given at the Council's October 2000 advocacy seminar in Phoenix, Arizona. Topics include responding to student threats, current issues of students with disabilities, the Family Educational Rights and Privacy Act (FERPA), e-mail and access to public meetings and records, the latest on prayer in schools, the Equal Access Act and related issues, legal considerations in measures to prevent school safety, hiring and retaining superintendents, responding to temporary restraining orders (TRO-s), high stakes testing, disciplining employees for off-campus conduct, private businesses and schools, race as a factor in student assignment, Cincinnati's alternative dispute resolution process, and do not resuscitate orders and other issues related to medically fragile students. 628 pages. ISBN 0-88364-241-7 (List $200, National Affiliates and Council Members $160).

School Law in Review 2001 (March 2001) This digest of papers presented at the 2001 Annual School Law Seminar includes religion in schools; prayer in schools; disciplining students for off campus Web sites; handling the errant board member; bilingual issues; school construction bidding issues; architects' contracts; conflicts of interest and the school attorney; impact of special education on extracurricular activities; and section 504 and student athletes. 190 pages. ISBN 0-88364-245-X (List $35, Council members - first copy free. National Affiliates and additional Council copies $28).

Selecting and Working With a School Attorney: A Guide for School Boards (April 1997) This publication shows school board members how to select and to work effectively with a school attorney. Topics include: historical development of the role of the school attorney, hiring in-house counsel vs. an outside attorney, selection, recruitment and retention of legal counsel, ethical issues in school board representation, evaluation and termination of school district counsel, the school attorney as a preventive law practitioner, how to work effectively with the school attorney. 142 pages. ISBN 0-88364-209-3 (List $35, National Affiliates and Council Members $28).

Sexual Harassment by School Employees (March 2001) Covering harassment that occurs between employees and employee harassment of students, this publication discusses current federal case law, effective policy development, how to conduct internal investigations, training advice and resources and agency (OCR and EEOC) investigations. The appendices contain many useful documents including regulations, agency guidance, sample policies and checklists. 228 pages. ISBN 0-88364-237-9 (List $35, National Affiliates and Council Members $28).

Student-to-Student Sexual Harassment: A Legal Guide for Schools (Revised Edition March 2000) This monograph provides the school law practitioner and school leaders with information on how to prevent, respond to, analyze and defend student to student harassment claims. It includes a section on policy development, advice on conducting investigation; tips for training, and analysis of the Office for and helpful check lists. 192 pages. ISBN 0-88364-235-2 (List $35, National Affiliates and Council Members $28).

Student Testing and Assessment: Answering the Legal Questions (September 2000) Among the materials included in this publication are an overview of state testing laws

and federal activity; a framework for making policy decisions about test use; discrimination and due process issues that may arise; considerations for testing special student groups, such as children with disabilities and limited English proficiency; and accountability of educators, schools and districts based on student test scores. 86 pages. ISBN 0-88364-239-5 (List $25, National Affiliates and Council Members $20).

Termination of School Employees: Legal Issues and Techniques (April 1997) This monograph addresses the legal issues and suggests effective techniques associated with proper termination of school employees. Topics include: employee performance documentation, evaluation, remediation, settlement agreements, public employee speech and off duty conduct, termination of drug/alcohol abusers, legal issues in trying a misconduct case, due process, and employment at will. 316 pages. ISBN 0-88364-210-7 (List $35, National Affiliates and Council Members $28).

The 1999 IDEA Regulations: A Practical Analysis (July 1999) This publication is a guide for all school professionals involved in special education to grasp the basic requirements and implications of the regulations issued by the U.S. Department of Education. Using an easy to follow format that tracks the regulations rule-by-rule, special education experts explain to you what you need to know and what you must do to comply with the provisions on a broad range of issues including: public charter schools, graduation of special needs students, assessments, use of Medicaid and insurance, IEP requirements, services to children in private schools, procedural safeguards, and discipline of children with disabilities. 96 pages. ISBN 0-88364-225-5 (List $25, National Affiliates and Council Members $20).

NSBA COUNCIL OF SCHOOL ATTORNEYS' PUBLICATION ORDER FORM
July 2001

SHIP TO: (Please provide street address, not P.O. Box)

Name _____

Title _____

Organization _____

Street Address _____

City _____ State _____ Zip _____

Phone (_____) _____

☐ My check made payable to NSBA in the amount of $_____ is enclosed.

☐ Bill me using P.O. Number _____
   PLEASE NOTE: Orders less than $30 must be paid in advance by check or credit card.

☐ My district is an NSBA National Affiliate,

   NA# _____

BILL TO: (if other than ship to)

Name _____

Title _____

Organization _____

Street Address _____

City _____ State _____ Zip _____

Phone (_____) _____

Please charge my: ☐ VISA ☐ MasterCard ☐ Amex

Card Number

_____

Authorized Signature   Exp. Date

☐ Check here to automatically receive new Council publications through the Standing Order System. I understand I have 30 days to preview publications and may return them at no risk, or I may keep them and submit payment.

Signature _____   Date _____

Order #	Title	Quantity	Member † Price	Nonmember Price	Total
New 06-182-1	**School Law in Review 2001 (back issues available)**		$28.00	$35.00	
New 06-181-1	**Religion & Public Schools: Striking a Constitutional Balance**		$28.00	$35.00	
New 06-176-1	**Sexual Harassment by School Employees**		$28.00	$35.00	
06-178-1	Student Testing and Assessment: Answering the Legal Questions		$20.00	$25.00	
06-177-1	Safe Schools, Safe Communities		$20.00	$25.00	
06-169-1	A School Law Primer: Part I Special Price for Purchasing Part I and Part II		$320.00 $512.00	$400.00 $640.00	
06-175-1	A School Law Primer: Part II Special Price for Purchasing Part I and Part II		$320.00 $512.00	$400.00 $640.00	
06-166A-1	Student-to-Student Sexual Harassment: A Legal Guide for Schools		$28.00	$35.00	
06-171-1	Desk Reference on Significant U.S. Supreme Court Decisions Affecting Public Schools		$20.00	$25.00	

Order #	Title	Quantity	Member † Price	Nonmember Price	Total
06-163-1	Termination of School Employees: Legal Issues and Techniques		$28.00	$35.00	
06-162-1	Selecting and Working With a School Attorney: A Guide for School Boards		$28.00	$35.00	
06-160-1	Legal Handbook on School Athletics		$28.00	$35.00	
06-158-1	School Reform: The Legal Challenges of Change		$25.00	$30.00	
06-156-1	Reasonable Accommodation of Disabled Employees: A Comprehensive Case Law Reference		$12.00	$15.00	
06-152-1	Legal Guidelines for Curbing School Violence		$25.00	$30.00	
06-151-1	Environmental Law: Fundamentals for Schools		$12.00	$15.00	
06-127-1	Contracting with Architects: A School District's Perspective		$20.00	$25.00	
06-148-1	Child Abuse: Legal Issues for Schools		$20.00	$25.00	
06-142-1	Americans with Disabilities Act: Its Impact on Public Schools		$20.00	$25.00	
06-136-1	School Board Member Liability Under Section 1983		$12.00	$15.00	
06-125-1	School Law Library Filing System		$12.00	$15.00	
03-145-10	Legal Issues & Education Technology: A School Leader's Guide		$28.00	$35.00	

Advocacy Notebooks —

New

Order #	Title	Quantity	Member † Price	Nonmember Price	Total
06-180-1	2000 Advocacy Seminar Notebook (October 2000) Phoenix, Arizona		$160.00	$200.00	
06-172-1	A School Law Retreat Advocacy Notebook (October 1999) Charleston, South Carolina		$160.00	$200.00	
06-167-1	A School Law Retreat Advocacy Notebook (October 1998) San Antonio, Texas		$160.00	$200.00	

† Member price is extended to NSBA Council of School Attorneys' members and NSBA National Affiliate School Districts.

Subtotal*

Shipping/Handling Charges

4.5% Sales tax (Va. Residents)

TOTAL

SHIPPING AND HANDLING CHARGES
(to All U.S. Zip-Coded Areas Only)

$ AMOUNT OF ORDER	SURFACE SHIPPING CHARGE
Up to $100.00	$7.00
$100.01 & Above	7% of order Total

Return this form to: NSBA Distribution Center
P.O. Box 161
Annapolis Jct., MD 20701

To order by phone
call NSBA at 800/706-6722, or
FAX form to 301/604-0158

Publications from the National School Boards Association's ITTE: Education Technology Programs

Special Reports

NEW! Technology Professional Development for P - 12 Educators (2001) Softbound. Get help planning, implementing, and assessing technology-related professional development for teachers and administrators in your district. This practical, user-friendly guide gives you research-based frameworks for designing staff development programs that are linked to student learning goals, incorporate new technology standards, and reflect adult learning theory. Funding strategies and sources, program profiles, and helpful resources are included.

$35 ($28 for TLN members)   Order # 03-149-44

NEW! Legal Issues & Education Technology: A School Leader's Guide, 2nd Edition (2001) Softbound. Written by members of NSBA's Council of School Attorneys (COSA), this guide emphasizes preventive strategies and knowledge school leaders need to avoid costly, disruptive litigation as they attempt to successfully blend various technologies into the instructional and administrative work of schools. Contents reflect recent legislation and court decisions and are presented in accessible format and language. Topics include: Internet filters; legal requirements for accessible Web design and ergonomically sound facilities; student and staff privacy rights; COPPA, CIPA, FERPA, ADA compliance issues and updates; copyright; acceptable use policies; off-site data storage policies; commercial agreements with e-businesses; open-meeting "sunshine" laws; and more.

$35 ($28 for TLN members)   Order # 03-150-44

Plans & Policies for Technology in Education: A Compendium, 2nd Edition (2000) Softbound, 238 pp. Actual district technology plans illustrate practical solutions school technology leaders have taken to address persistent problems in education technology integration. The second edition supplements the resources included in the first edition of *Plans & Policies*, featuring 25 new district plans and updated information on trends and issues. The guide features a user-friendly six-step planning model, articulates a conceptual framework for technology planning, offers nuts-and-bolts guidelines for developing action plans, and provides extensive examples and discussion of acceptable use policies, facilities management, staff development, curriculum integration, and other critical topics. Also included are abundant Internet and other resources for technology planners.
$35 ($28 for TLN members)   Order # 03-147-44

Plans & Policies for Technology in Education: A Compendium, 1st Edition (1995) Softbound, 250 pp. This compilation of plans from 38 districts presents detailed examples of strategies, policies, and plans implemented by a variety of large and small districts. Topics include: purchasing, copyright, network/Internet use, ethics,

staff development, curricular integration, technology access, equity, community involvement, evaluation, and more.

$35 ($28 for TLN members)   Order # 03-133-44

SPECIAL OFFER Save 20% on the *Plans & Policies* set: Get the first and second editions of *Plans & Policies* for one low price!

$56 ($45 for TLN members)   Order# 03-148-44

Models of Success: Case Studies of Technology in Schools (1999) Softbound, 232 pp. In this exciting collection of case studies, planning and policy documents appear alongside narratives of what 20 school districts have achieved with technology. Chapters divide the studies according to how education leaders have used technology to support student achievement, technology infrastructure, professional development, and community-wide learning. Developed with support from Microsoft Corporation, the models, documents, contacts, and guidance help readers construct and refine their own success stories.

$35 ($28 for TLN members)   Order # 03-146-44

Leader's Guide to Education Technology (1998) Softbound, 24 pp. Research, analysis, and recommendations included in this volume help you make sound technology decisions about student achievement, educational equity, and work force preparedness. You'll find empirical evidence of how technology makes a difference in teaching and learning as well as examples of the challenges schools face and sample questions to ask when considering technology planning. A good guide to give others who need to "get on board" the school improvement effort, it is published by the EDvancenet project—a partnership of the National School Boards Foundation, the Consortium for School Networking, and MCI WorldCom—and is also available at www.edvancenet.org.

$10 ($8 for TLN members)   Order # 03-144-44

Technology & School Design: Creating Spaces for Learning (1998) Softbound, 122 pp. This essential guide will help you plan and design or remodel school buildings, hire skilled architects and technology consultants, and work to create effective learning spaces. Written by leading school architects and technology consultants, it will be instrumental as you develop technology plans and make upgrades to your school and district infrastructure.

$35 ($28 for TLN members)   Order # 03-143-44

Investing in School Technology: Strategies to Meet the Funding Challenge/School Leader's Version (1997) Softbound, 85 pp. Learn more sophisticated costing and budgeting techniques to finance technology in your school district. Supported by Newcourt Credit Group and based on a report prepared for the U.S. Department of Education, the "School Leader's Version" also supplies a glossary and information on additional funding sources.

$25 ($20 for TLN members)   Order# 03-140-44

Technology for Students with Disabilities: A Decision Maker's Resource Guide (1997) Softbound, 103 pp. Technology is an essential ally in helping students who have learning problems, major cognitive disabilities, or physical disabilities. This guide offers strategies for technology implementation to improve curriculum, assessment, and administration. Readers find assistance in assessing their needs; choosing and funding technology; and creating policy frameworks, long-range technology plans, and due process procedures. Relevant federal documents are reprinted along with an extensive resource list (also available at www.nsba.org/itte). Published by NSBA and the U.S. Department of Education's Office of Special Education Programs.
$25 ($20 for TLN members)   Order# 03-138-44

Education Leadership Toolkit: A Desktop Companion (1997) Softbound, 32 pp. This is a concise introduction to many of the issues education leaders face as they integrate technology into their districts' activities and operations. Designed to prompt discussion and exploration, the *Desktop Companion* is divided into scenarios with questions to consider, followed by tips and resources for developing an approach to navigating the wealth of material available at the Education Leadership Toolkit Web site at www.nsba.org/sbot/toolkit.
$10 ($8 for TLN members)   Order# 03-142-44

Leadership & Technology: What School Board Members Need to Know (1995) Softbound, 194 pp. To ask the right questions and make appropriate policy decisions, school board members need to consider and understand the wide array of technology-related issues that are treated here in a discussion guide format. Also find a step-by-step guide to technology planning, advice about the board's relationship to administrators and the district's technology planning committee, a glossary of terms, and a bibliography.
$35 ($28 for TLN members)   Order# 03-135-44

Multimedia and Learning: A School Leader's Guide (1994) Softbound, 116 pp. Learn how to improve teaching and learning experiences through the use of multimedia and to address related issues such as facility planning, staff development, copyright, and learning theory. Glossary included.
$35 ($28 for TLN members)   Order# 03-129-44

Newsletter
Technology Leadership News is an eight-page newsletter published nine times a year as a membership benefit for the superintendent and designated personnel in Technology Leadership Network (TLN) districts. TLN members may order additional subscriptions at 50% off the regular price. Members may also access the newsletter at the ITTE Web site using the membership user name and passcode.
$100 per year ($50 for TLN members)   Order# 03-119-44

To Order
To order publications or for more information, call the NSBA Distribution Center at 1-800-706-6722, or complete the order form at the end of this section and mail or fax your order to NSBA.

ITTE: Education Technology Programs and its Technology Leadership Network

To order please complete this order form
and return it by mail to NSBA Distribution Center, P.O. Box 161, Annapolis Jct., MD 20701-0161.
To order by phone, call NSBA at 800-706-6722. To order by FAX, dial NSBA at 301-604-0158.

SHIP TO: (Street address—all orders sent UPS)

Name _____

Title _____

Organization _____

Street Address _____

City_____ State _____ Zip _____

Phone (_____) _____

BILL TO: (if other than ship to)

Name _____

Title _____

Organization _____

Street Address _____

City_____ State _____ Zip _____

Phone (_____) _____

Title	Quantity	Discount Price*	Regular Price	Total
Technology Professional Development for P-12 Educators 03-149-44		$28.00	$35.00	
Legal Issues & Education Technology: A School Leader's Guide 2nd Edition 03-150-44		$28.00	$35.00	
Plans & Policies for Technology in Education: A Compendium 2nd Edition 03-147-44		$28.00	$35.00	
Models of Success: Case Studies of Technology in Schools 03-146-44		$28.00	$35.00	
Leader's Guide to Education Technology 03-144-44		$8.00	$10.00	
Technology & School Design: Creating Spaces for Learning 03-143-44		$28.00	$35.00	
Education Leadership Toolkit: A Desktop Companion 03-142-44		$8.00	$10.00	
Investing in School Technology: Strategies to Meet the Funding Challenge 03-140-44		$20.00	$25.00	
Technology for Students with Disabilities: A Decision Maker's Resource Guide 03-138-44		$20.00	$25.00	
Leadership & Technology: What School Board Members Need to Know 03-135-44		$28.00	$35.00	
Plans & Policies for Technology in Education: A Compendium 03-133-44		$28.00	$35.00	
Electronic School 03-101-25-44 (To receive latest issue)		$4.00	$5.00	
Multimedia and Learning: A School Leader's Guide 03-129-44		$28.00	$35.00	
Plans and Policies set 03-148-44		$45.00	$56.00	
Technology Leadership News (9 issues annually) 03-119-44		TLN Benefit	$100.00	
			SUBTOTAL:	
		SHIPPING AND HANDLING: (see charges below)		
			TOTAL:	

❐ My check made payable to NSBA in the amount
of $ _____ is enclosed.

❐ Bill me using P.O. # _____
($20 minimum order)

Please charge my: ❐ VISA   ❐ MasterCard   ❐ American Express

Card Number _____

Expiration Date _____

Name (please print) _____

Authorized Signature _____

For more information about NSBA's technology publications contact
Ismat Abdal-Haqq at NSBA, 1680 Duke St., Alexandria, VA 22314,
(703) 838-6214, e-mail: iabdal-haqq@nsba.org. For information
about NSBA's National Affiliate Program, contact Bonita Metz at
that address, (703) 838-6746, e-mail: bmetz@nsba.org.

* These publications are discounted to NSBA National Affiliate
and Technology Leadership Network districts.
To receive this discount you must check one of the spaces below:

❐ My district is a National Affiliate, # _____

❐ My district participates in the Technology Leadership
Network.

Shipping and Handling Charges
(to all US Zip-Coded Areas only)
$ Amount of Order ....**Surface Shipping Charge**
up to $100.00...........................$7.00
$100.01 - and above.................7% of total order

Shipping and handling charges for Canadian/overseas orders will
be billed at $7.00 plus actual postage. Quantity discounts available; for information call 800-706-6722.

Visit us on the Web!
See Tables of Contents and more at
http://www.nsba.org/itte/publicat.html

Order Form

To receive 9 issues of Technology Leadership News per year for only $100, complete this order form and mail or fax to NSBA.· · · · · · · · · · · · · · · · ·

Special Offer for Technology Leadership Network Members ~ 50% discount Only $50 per year

Technology Leadership News
ITTE: Education Technology Programs
National School Boards Association
1680 Duke Street
Alexandria, VA 22314
phone: 703-838-6214
fax: 703-548-5516

Technology Leadership Network District _____

SHIP TO:
Name _____
Title _____
Organization _____
Street Address _____
City _____ State _____ Zip _____
Phone (_____) _____ Fax (_____) _____
E-mail _____

BILL TO:
Name _____
Title _____
Organization _____
Street Address _____
City _____ State _____ Zip _____
Phone (_____) _____ Fax (_____) _____
E-mail _____

❏ My check, payable to NSBA, in the amount of $_____ is enclosed.
❏ Bill me using P.O. # _____.
Please charge my: ❏ VISA ❏ MasterCard ❏ American Express
Card Number _____ Expiration Date _____
Name (please print) _____
Authorized Signature _____

ITTE ONLY
03-119_____ Billing Code _____

February 2001
TLNews order form